Monkey
taming

JUDITH
FATHALLAH

DEFINITIONS

MONKEY TAMING
A DEFINITIONS BOOK 9780099488453

Published in Great Britain by Definitions
an imprint of Random House Children's Books

This edition published 2006

5 7 9 10 8 6 4

The Random House Group Limited makes every effort to ensure that the
papers used in its books are made from trees that have been legally
sourced from well-managed and credibly certified forests. Our paper
procurement policy can be found at:
www.randomhouse.co.uk/paper.htm

Set in New Baskerville by Palimpsest Book Production Limited,
Polmont, Stirlingshire

Definitions are published by Random House Children's Books,
61–63 Uxbridge Road, London W5 5SA,
a division of The Random House Group Ltd

Addresses for companies within The Random House Group Limited
can be found at: www.randomhouse.co.uk/offices.htm

THE RANDOM HOUSE GROUP Limited Reg. No. 954009
www.**kids**at**randomhouse**.co.uk

A CIP catalogue record for this book is available from the British Library

Printed and bound in Great Britain by
Cox & Wyman Ltd, Reading, Berkshire

Sincere thanks go to Sarah Manson, agent, and to Charlie Sheppard and the Random House team. It has been a delight and a learning experience to work with you. Also to my many friends amongst the staff and pupils of St David's College, for continuous support and encouragement to pursue my dream.

Judith Fathallah suffered from anorexia nervosa when she was 13. She has now made a full recovery and is studying English at Cambridge where she is particularly interested in Renaissance and Twentieth-century literature. She still loves writing.

'To remember everything is a form of madness'

Brian Friel, *Translations*

PART ONE:
GROWING

chapter one

'You've eaten too much, you fat pig.'

I can tell where it started. Not *when* it started, because these things don't start like a thunderbolt out of the blue. They're more like water, building up behind a dam, and you feel it but you can't do much to stop it. Then the dam breaks. *Whoosh.*

My dam broke in Germany. It was July, a holiday, the painful sort of family holiday you do to pretend things are OK and you're happy when they're actually pretty screwed. I was thirteen, I was self-obsessed. There were deeper struggles going on at that time in the old family unit, but for me the badness, the uncomfortable feeling, all honed in on one problem.

I was fat.

We'd been swimming at the Atlantis pool complex. I used the time to scrutinize dozens of bikini-clad German girls, and feel horrible. *If I could look like them,* I thought, *things would be fine. If I could only get slim I could cope with*

3

everything. At 10 stone 1 pound and 5 foot 2 inches, my size and shape were growing on my mind. Literally. I would try on numerous outfits every morning and inspect myself in the mirror, perturbed at the size of my tummy, hips and thighs. Putting on my swimsuit for the first time in months had been a nightmare.

As we left Atlantis, my mum started to describe this whale of a woman she'd seen at the side of the pool:

'She was sitting there with this picnic basket, and she just kept eating out of it, her hand going back and forth, back and forth. Sandwich, sandwich, piece of cake. She wanted to stop but she couldn't. You could tell she wanted to stop because she kept closing the lid as if to say, *OK, that's enough now*, but then five minutes later she'd open it again! Then the daughter came out of the pool to eat and—'

'Was the daughter fat?' I interrupted.

'Well, she was all right, I suppose, but she looked as though she could be going that way,' Mum replied.

'Fatter than me?' I wanted to know.

'Yes, fatter than— Well, maybe she was like you.'

I scowled. So! I looked as though I could be going that way too, did I? Well, yes, probably. But what could I do about it? This was me. I had always been fat and always would be. Dairylea Triangles were comfort.

'I hate being so fat,' I moaned. This had been my parrot-call for many months, and my mum was clearly sick of it. Not for the first time, she suggested that I try to do something about it.

'I'll support you, Jess,' she enthused. 'I know how to do it! Get active! Go swimming! You used to go swimming all the time. I know how to cook healthy food. I used to weigh eight stone.'

It's true – I've seen cine-film of my mother as a young woman and she really was fantastically slim and glamorous. In fact, she always looked a bit on the skinny side to me.

'If you really want to lose weight,' she continued, 'I know how to do it – but don't just go on about it all the time.'

My least favourite emotion is guilt, but humiliation comes a close second. Red-faced, eyes-narrowed, smouldering humiliation. I was proud. I still am about some things, but I'm trying to be better. And stupid as it was, I felt humiliated. My plump cheeks burned. It was a reasonable, supportive suggestion but I took it badly. A small, hard resentment-seed took root inside my stomach, like an orange pip.

OK, I thought. *I will get slim. Really slim. As slim as all my friends. I'll show everyone just how slim I can get, and just how fast I can get there.*

This was not the first time I had made that resolution. Many times over the past year, usually lying in bed late at night, I had resolved that this was it – there would be no more pizza, no more ice creams, or any of the other naughty things I added to our healthy home-inventory of food. But somehow my hard will had always dissolved by the morning. The breakfast-time pull of French bread with ham and cheese, to combat the creeping dull depression that was grasping at me, always proved too strong.

This time, though, my resolution stuck. It stuck through the night and through all the next day. It stuck while I wandered dazedly around Heidelberg. I have absolutely no idea what that city looks like, save a vague impression that it's tall, and there are department stores there. I was glowering inside. I spent the guided coach tour arranging my legs to look as not-fat as they possibly could and flicking the controls on my headphones from English to French to Scandinavian and back again. My resolve even stuck while I ate half a sandwich and a few bites of apple for lunch, and refused the chocolate my mum bought later that day.

'But, Jess!' my brother protested, 'it's *anorexic*, the amount you've eaten today!' We laughed.

But as my laughter faded, something unexpected

happened. A small, pleasing thing. A little voice piped up inside me suddenly:

'Good going, Jess! There's some willpower – you're eating like a thin person already.'

I had some grapes for tea on the way back to our hotel, and I didn't feel hungry. No one said anything else; I had been sullen, moody and estranged for months. I suppose they thought it was just the latest fad.

The next night I pigged out on Pringles. Salt-and-vinegar flavour. *What the hell*, I thought. *I'm on holiday!*

Look at me! I laughed at myself as I lounged on the white hotel sheets. *I just decided to diet yesterday and I've already messed it up!*

'Well obviously,' said the voice, sardonic now. *'As if you'd ever really get slim.'*

It was a crappy hotel. You had to go down the corridor in the night to get to the toilet, or else you had to pee in the bath. We had booked somewhere else, but they had no record of our reservation. Fun. But we pretended that it was good and that we were happy, because we were struggling inside.

Throughout the rest of that holiday we took more exercise than I was used to. Walking, swimming, cycling. I kept my little idea in mind, and opted for a salad when we went to restaurants, feeling very adult and superior. If I did have a piece of cake I made sure it replaced a meal. My favourite kind had raspberry jelly inside and moist chocolate sponge on the bottom: delicious. Sure enough, when we returned home, my holiday trousers felt a little looser.

'Jessica,' said Mum conversationally, 'I'm *sure* you've lost weight this holiday – why don't you weigh yourself and find out?'

I shook my head. The scales were not my friend, and I had learned long ago that it was best not to try them and upset myself. Same principle as diet and exercise, really.

'Oh go on,' said Mum, and I was curious.

We were standing in the bathroom, sorting washing, and the scales were just lying there, looking so innocent. What harm could that one little white box possibly do? I decided to give it a try.

'I'm nine stone ten!' I cried, delighted.

'Oh, Jessica, you *have* lost weight!' Mum was pleased for me too.

'And I'm going to carry on,' I announced, beaming.

'OK,' said Mum, 'and I'll support you.'

It was the middle of August.

The dam had burst.

chapter two

I am half Arab. My father came from Syria, so my name is Jessica Hassan. I had a lovely childhood. Idyllic, like on television. Me, my mum, my dad, my older brother Adam and the cat. With guest appearances from Nan.

They say the first few years of your life form your personality. Family is the shield for future shock. That might well be erring on the side of bullshit, but I'm certainly glad to have had those years, if only because they're fun to look back on. What came afterwards was, in part, an attempt to reclaim my lost childhood.

The five of us (including the cat, not the nan) lived in a terraced house. I liked our street, because a lot of children lived in the houses there. We could play outside during the summer. An adult would stand in a doorway, keeping an eye on us, and our parents knew we were safe.

I went to the local primary school. It was a good school. We had hopscotch painted on the playground, and when it rained, there was a puddle there that looked exactly like a whale.

They made a fuss of me for being clever in that primary school, and because I could write. I've always written. In reception class the other kids still gripped the pencil in their fists. I was churning out three-page stories.

I have lots of faults: I'm proud; I can be hard and jealous and occasionally still selfish, though I have been humbled. But I *am* clever, and that's just stating a fact. It's genetic. My brother is too, and my mum; and my father was the cleverest of us all.

My dad was warm and kind. I used to be warmer and kinder. When I was small it seemed he had about a hundred friends, many of them Arabs, and there were frequent gatherings at our house with lots of laughter. Then I was lifted up to be admired, and to charm the company with my precocious cheeky tongue and head of curly hair. I revelled in adulation. I liked to sit cross-legged on the floor in the middle of the living room, listening to their mingled-language talk:

'Grarrar rarrar washing machine rar.' It made me laugh. One of these Arab men was bald, and used to joke that I had stolen all his hair until I screeched with laughter. One day I made him some fake hair: a strip of paper, crayoned brown, to attach to his head with Sellotape. They all loved it. And, of course, there was food there – scrumptious, fattening Arabic food, with names I can't think how to spell. Those days smell like spice and taste like meaty sauces. There was a yellow rice with raisins in. My dad used to eat that at Christmas while we had our roast potatoes. I asked why, and they wondered if I could guess.

'Go on then,' said Mum jokingly. 'Let's see how sensitive she is.'

I hadn't a clue, but they didn't realize I knew what *sensitive* meant. It clicked.

'Daddy misses Syria,' I pronounced.

I was warmly applauded. Everywhere was love, for I loved everyone around this table, and this table and this warmth and this house comprised the whole of the world.

Then, when I was nine, the world shattered.

Some days are emblazoned in your mind, no matter how much you wish you could forget them. So, uselessly, I know that I was wearing blue jeans and a purple jumper on that seventeenth of November, know we'd had jacket potatoes for tea, and that the cat was in a mood because Adam had stepped on his tail. I know that it was twenty past six in the evening when

11

the doorbell rang, and that I answered the door.

What do you do when you see police officers, with their sombre, concerned expressions? (One of them is always a woman – they send women along to tell these things; it's some kind of secret rule.) What do you do when your dad is late home from work and you haven't even been worried about him, and now, now you know, beyond the shadow of a doubt, that while you have been eating your jacket potato and tuna fish, talking and laughing, he was already dead?

This was November the seventeenth.

Car crash, instant death, fault of the other driver. Both dead. No one could have survived it. Not even anyone left to hate, left to blame, just – this emptiness.

Really, what do you do?

This is what my mother did. Very late that night – or maybe by then it was morning – she sat on the floor, with one arm around each of her children. And she said, 'We *will* be all right. I want you to know that. We have each other, we're not going to lose the house. We *will* be all right.' Then we wept.

Three months afterwards, when I was back at school, two girls approached me wide-eyed in the corridor and asked in a tone of awe, 'Is your dad *dead*?'

'Yes,' said my voice. For once, rumour was true. I was

the girl whose father was dead: an object of horror and awe.

But the years still turned, and we survived, and maybe there is no getting over, but there is getting through. And there were birthday parties, and barbecues, and a kitten that grew into a cat. And then, one day, there was laughter again, although the tone was jaded. And I learned to do things with my mother, like shopping, instead of riding bikes with my dad: it was not the same, would never be the same, but it was a new thing altogether, and it came to be complete in itself. She didn't hug and kiss me like he did – that just wasn't her way – but I knew she loved me, and maybe I didn't need kisses so much any more, because I was getting older. So we were three, a different three, no longer four-with-a-hole-in.

Of course, the loss would never go away. A handful of years is nothing. At any moment, I could draw up the pain, wrenching, chasm-like, and be nine years old again, and know the meaning of agony. Or be six, hold his hand, and be taken to see the planes lift off at the runway, smell his aftershave, now pain-ridden. The continuum between me and that girl was oddly broken, but I could jump that break whenever I wanted. As time passed, I chose to retreat there less often. We aged, but he didn't: he would always be forty-two, immortalized by a smiling photograph in a frame on the study wall.

The new three moved to a different house, and remained as three until my grandmother came to live with us. She came because she was ill, with Parkinson's disease and developing dementia. It began with stiff muscles and forgetfulness, but by the time I was twelve she could hardly walk, or speak clearly, or remember my name. Sometimes she would almost seem her old self; other times she saw strange things, like cats upside down on the ceiling, or children in the corner. That could be pretty funny:

'It's that child, the one with the flowers again.' And I would actually look.

But sometimes she saw dark things, frightening things for which she had no name. She could be vicious:

'You always were a bad egg, you.'

'It's just me, Nan. It's Jess.'

'Oh yes,' in a tone of knowing scepticism, as though we were all out to trick her. When my mum tried to give her her medicine:

'*Poison!*' she'd shriek, and clamp her lips shut like a vice. Other times, she sang. Hymns mostly, or popular songs from the thirties. Her cracked, reedy voice parodied the notes, and she swayed as she sang.

One night I'd just been starting to drift off to sleep when my door thudded open. My mother stood silhouetted in the doorway, hair messed up and a panicky light in her eyes.

'Jess,' she said, fumbling with her keys as I sat bolt upright. Light flooded in from the hallway. 'I have to go out.'

'What?' My heart was hammering. *That's it. She's lost it. Well, I'm screwed now.*

'Adam's stuck at the bus station. The service has been cancelled.'

'But – she – I can't—'

'Jess, I'll be fifteen minutes. Just stay here. You don't have to go to her.'

'But—'

My mother did something out of character. She rushed over and kissed me spontaneously, on the forehead. Then she left. The slamming of the front door sent shivers through me.

I sat there in semi-darkness, clutching the covers around me. Time passed, measured only by the thudding of my heart inside my head. And then it came. The inevitable—

'Laura? Laura?' – my mother's name – and then, horribly: '*Jack!*'

Jack was her husband, my mother's father. He died twenty years before I was born. The cries to the ghost continued: '*Jack! Jack!*' and then shadows lurched in the doorway as she clambered, haltingly, to her feet. On reflex I started up – *Oh God, she'll fall down the stairs* – but then I froze again as I heard her stumble against the bookcase. There was a creak, then a smash as an ornament broke on the floor.

'Where is it? What have they done with it?'

Smash, smash. I watched the stretching shadows of the small green china ladies as they toppled and exploded into shards.

'*Ja-ack!*' she wailed again. I would have to go to her. Heart pounding, I shoved my feet into my trainers and slipped out into the awful light.

My grandmother stood hunched and awkward, clawing her way through ornaments and photographs – my Year Four class picture clattered face-down to the ground.

'Nan!' I cried, half-reaching towards her, and she turned – looked through me with film-covered eyes, mouth open and trembling in fear. I stepped back in shock at that face, for the woman was gone; I was meeting a ghost, just a shell and a shivering ghost. I was backing away – couldn't help myself – when she pointed a crooked yellow finger at me and squawked, '*You!*'

Now she saw me, or saw something in the place where I was standing. She called me no name – and I'd heard some bad ones – but the accusation in that voice, the repulsion, the sheer *hate*: had I ever heard hate before?

'It's me, Nan.' I spread my hands. 'It's only Jess.'

She lurched towards me and fell, hard, landing on slivers of china. A wail of pain spilled out of her. I screamed and made to run for the phone – but just at that moment, my mother's key turned in the door.

Nan had broken her hip in the fall, and after that she couldn't walk at all. She was in hospital for three weeks, and one of the doctors suggested we start to look for a nursing home.

'I want to try at home one more time first,' said my mother adamantly; so from then on she was pretty much a full-time carer.

No longer could I come home and report my latest A grade, or receive assurance that the kids who called me swot or fatso were just jealous. No more family dinners – what had happened to the three? No more cinema at weekends – and the nights! The nights were worst of all. Five or six times, Nan would shout, 'Laura! Laura!' or worse: 'Help! *Heeeeeelp!*' and up my mother would get, and I would lie there listening and feeling worried that she wasn't getting any sleep and guilty that I couldn't be of more help. This alternated with jealousy:

'I haven't seen you all day! Why don't you have any time for me?' This was after a particularly bad day at high school, when some kids thought it would be a laugh to steal my bag, spilling my papers, and throw it around above my head in the yard. Piggy-in-the-middle indeed – of course I was too short and fat to stand a chance of retrieving it – and I arrived home hot, tearful and missing six pages of French homework. My mother knew nothing of this.

'You think I enjoy this?' She stood at the bottom of the stairs, looking tired and angry.

'No . . .'

'Laura! Laura! *Heeeelp!*'

My mother's face almost crumpled. Horrified at myself, furious with my grandmother, I hurried up to my bedroom. Closed the door and sat down on the floor. I did nothing for several minutes. The weird tragic wails of: 'You're trying to kill me!' easily pierced the walls. Accepting this background noise, I began to redo my French.

Adam didn't like to talk about sad things. He was out of the house a lot. When he came in, he shut himself up in his bedroom and played on his computer. I never saw him cry.

I was getting fatter. Long hours alone to fill between school-end and bedtime. The fridge for company. Dairylea Triangles. Two, three. Then half the packet. I was guilty for a while – then what did it matter? Who cared if I was fat? Something fast and easy for tea, which my mother or I could just pop in the oven: chicken burgers or pizza. Lie on the couch and feel bad.

If only Dad were here.

chapter three

When we got back from that holiday in Germany, I resolved to slim down a bit more for the start of the school year. The very thought of returning to school frustrated me: *that crappy place.* I never really got over the disappointment of beginning high school. I was a nonentity there, another faceless object to be levered through exams. Sure, the odd teacher took an interest in me, when they could get time between marking and the other pressures of an overstressed job. But I was one of many when I once had been a star. Lessons, boring. Disrupted and disordered. Bags thrown across the classroom, teachers dull-eyed, looking at their watches. Screechy dinner ladies saying, '*Get out!*' when it was pissing down with rain. Puke-coloured corridors. The shrill bell. High school. And yes, of course I got called fat.

I had friends – well, *a* friend. Rachel was the only person I still really cared about.

'You're not fat,' she would reassure me after I'd been teased, or sometimes: 'It doesn't matter what you look like anyway, Jess. Some people are so shallow.'

Well, that's stupid, I thought in sudden irritation. *A minute ago she said I wasn't fat. Now she's suggesting I am, which is right of course. It just goes to show you can't trust what people tell you.* But she was still my companion, and I still needed her around.

Mum agreed it might give me a boost to lose half a stone or so before the new school year began. Once I started, it turned out I was rather good at losing weight. I ate healthy, balanced meals and began to swim lengths three times a week. *Well,* I thought, glancing at the pool clock after a first exhausting session, *that was about forty-five minutes,* and I left the pool.

Things were looking up. Still three weeks left before school, and Nan went into a home at last, my mother admitting unhappily that she couldn't cope any longer. Perhaps it would've been easier had I not been so desperate for attention. One day of doctors going in and out of the house and the phone ringing constantly, and then she was gone. My mother visited her often. I didn't. I told myself I would, someday in the future. When I was slim and could cope. Now my mother cooked slimming food for me like fish, vegetables and salads. Our house had always been one of low-fat spreads and lean mince, with McDonald's reserved as an occasional treat. It was only while Nan was with us that good habits had given way to convenience.

Nine stone four. A week before school started, I was nine stone four and squeezing into a size twelve. Sitting at the computer, playing Dungeon Keeper, I listened to Mum arranging our next family visit to London, to visit the uncles there. They were my dad's brothers and we still went to see them quite often. Summer visits meant a barbecue in the back yard, and the garden pool.

'And I can't *wait* for you to see Jessica,' Mum told the relative on the line. 'She's lost a *stone* almost, and she looks lovely.'

So when I visited London, I was showered with compliments. I lapped them up, glowing. I was really getting somewhere now. I was going to be a star again. Noticed, praised, smiled upon. This was what I needed, this was going to bring me happiness. But those four pounds stuck out like a sore thumb, irritating me. If I could lose just five more, I would be *eight stone something*. Who'd have thought it?

When school began again, the scales were flickering between nine four and nine two. On the actual day I went back, the scales read nine stone four.

'It would've been nice if I could have been feeling slim for my first day back at school.' I was sulking.

'Well, *feeling* slim is the key word,' replied Mum. 'Because you can't tell. Weight fluctuates, and people are going to tell you you've lost weight.'

Yes! Perhaps they would! How wonderful that would be. Surely even my tormentors must look twice now, see I wasn't such a loser after all. I took extra care with my hair that morning, twisting it up and pinning it, and put on a little mascara. Regarded myself in the mirror, heart beating. Different. My cheeks were not as chubby as they had been, and for the first time in my life I could see the line of my cheekbones.

'Hiya,' said Rachel when I opened the front door.

I beamed.

'Let's go then,' she said.

'I've lost a stone.' Perhaps she just needed a little pointer.

'Oh, have you? Well done. Hey, did we have homework for Mrs Holloway?'

I blinked. Well. Well, OK. Rachel was Rachel: appearances had never mattered to her. That was what was so *good* about her – she was genuine. Things would be different in class – they had to be. I entered Year Nine with my jaw set.

Nothing happened until maths class. No one even glanced my way. But then, as Mr Berkley wrote out long division questions on the whiteboard and students clattered and groaned, I heard my name whispered behind me and stiffened, waiting.

There was a long pause. Then 'Jessica' again, and giggles. My heart sank.

'Jess,' said Rachel quietly.

'What?'

'Sorry.' And she reached behind my head, and pulled out piece by piece a small assortment of pens, pencils and ripped-up bits of paper kids had poked into my thick hair – some of the paper was chewed up and spit-drenched. Some kind of betting game. *She's gonna notice now – no, now – go on, dare you to stick in one more pencil* . . . Compliment me? What had I been thinking? This was high school, for God's sake. Why did I listen to my mother? People didn't *compliment* you in high school, they just tormented you or bitched behind your back.

I carried on swimming, and one day it occurred to me that I'd had rather a lot of rests during my session. '*No good,*' that peculiar voice I'd been hearing from time to time piped up. '*Add extra minutes on at the end to compensate.*' And from then on I tried to make all my sessions forty-five minutes, breaks *not* included.

Then one day my weight skipped right on down to eight stone thirteen, totally ignoring nine stone. *Oh wow!* I thought. *Eight stone something! I made eight stone something!* It was so good to see that little red eight. Feelings of happiness – real, light happiness – were jumping around inside me. Hell, I'd almost forgotten them. This dieting was really something. I was onto a winner. I couldn't stop now, just when I was feeling better for the first time in ages. Schooldays dwindled in their power to depress me. I had a secret game going on now. I was above them.

It must have been around that time that I discovered calories. I discovered them in the form of a twenty-year-old pink and yellow booklet, shoved to the back of a kitchen drawer and collecting dust.

It told me the number of calories per ounce of pretty much any basic food, and I began to take notice of the little printed box on the back of packets and jars. I asked Mum for estimates of the calories in the meals she gave me, and clocked up the numbers in my head. According to the book, 1,000 to 1,500 calories a day was a slimming diet, depending on build, sex, energy expenditure and the amount of excess weight to be lost. 1,000 for me, then. To be safe.

Eight and a half stone. I glared at myself in the mirror.

Nobody made any comments on my weight any more, negative or positive, but I knew that I wasn't slim. Just look at the bulge of my stomach, my thighs! *'Disgusting! Too fat! There's only one thing to do,'* the voice advised sagely. *'Let's take it down to eight.'*

I decided I needed more exercise, so I took up dancing. I shut my bedroom door very firmly, put on some fast music and started.

'Jess, will you keep it *down*?' Adam banged on the door.

'Get lost!' I yelled over the beat. Nobody was going to stop this now, not when I was getting somewhere.

'I'm *trying* to watch the television!'

'And *I'm* doing something important!'

A few pounds over eight stone and I started to lose my appetite. My stomach was shrinking. Counting out my 1,000 calories became a chore, and often I'd get to 800 or so and just not want any more. Mum wasn't too happy with this, but agreed that as long as I didn't go under eight stone it didn't really matter. After all, I think we both thought, Mum was eight stone, and she's a good inch taller than me!

I got into the habit of fast dancing every day I didn't swim perfectly (forty-five minutes without stopping). I would get tired, carry on, stop being tired and pretend

I was a professional dancer, or part of a backing group for whatever band or singer I had on. I imagined I was on *Top of the Pops*, so I had to get it just right or I might mess up my big chance of being spotted and becoming a performer in my own right. I felt great afterwards: exhausted, exhilarated and in control.

In October I wore size ten jeans. But my weight was sticking at eight stone four, and I hated it. That four stuck out like an even bigger sore thumb than it had the last time, when I was a stone heavier; a horrible swollen sore thumb.

But it was the spot exercises that really roused the voice inside my head. I decided that as well as being slim I wanted a toned body. No point in doing things by halves. The evenings were growing short, cold and dark, and Mum was growing tired of taking me swimming. So she taught me to do sit-ups and things to replace some of my swims. Good things in themselves, strengthening. But my dark voice was growing too fast, and sometimes in the night, sheer panic gripped me as I felt it take over my control:

'*Don't be so stupid,*' it would reassure me harshly. '*You need me. I'm keeping you upright, keeping you on the straight and narrow, kid.*'

'*Of course, of course. I'll just sleep.*'

chapter four

There is a sense of great rapidity to all this. Even the professionals were surprised how fast I did it. But I did things fast and early as a rule. That could be good or bad.

Even Rachel commented now – on how well I'd done. Mum bought me a new top to match the jeans and I couldn't help feeling a tiny bit pleased as I observed my reflection. Not good enough – of course it wasn't good enough – but better. *'Don't be so vain,'* sneered the voice. *'For God's sake, look at your stomach. You shouldn't have eaten that yoghurt, you know – you could have gone without it.'* My mother told me I looked good, but I knew she, and everyone else, was lying. My weight slid continually down, but I couldn't stand the flickering of our digital scales – *What, did it say seven twelve? I saw seven ten yesterday!* 'You pig, you've put weight on!' The scales ruled my moods, and people noticed.

'Jess, you want to come see a film with me?' Adam asked.

'No.'

'Why don't we hang out together any more?' He sounded hurt and confused.

'Cos I'm busy.'

'Doing what?

'Stuff! You wouldn't understand!' *You're skinny and you don't even try. It's not fair. If I was as skinny as you I could eat whatever I wanted.*

'Jess, you've changed.' Adam gave me a long, sober look. 'You used to be a laugh. Now you're either really miserable or really giggly and stupid' – i.e. fat days and less-fat days.

This was very odd: I liked to think I handled everything myself now, and didn't know my feelings were so obvious. I put it all down to the unreliable scales. That had to be it. Once I was slim, the numbers wouldn't matter so much; then surely I'd return to having a good relationship with my family.

Eventually, I persuaded Mum to replace the digital scales with some brand-new dial ones, and I was on tenterhooks until they arrived.

I exercised religiously: spot exercises five times a day. I pulled the number five out of the air. No one had told me how many times I should do them per day, so I guessed. I thought five sounded nice and regular, and not too few. I liked to be certain about things. Trouble is, obsessions never lead to certainty. Afterwards I would think that half of the exercises were incorrect and didn't count, so I would do them again. And again. The morning session was making me late for school. So I started getting up earlier.

Time to weigh and measure was the first thought in my brain. *Or should I exercise first? No, reap yesterday's rewards before beginning the day's work.* In retrospect, it seems ugly. Pathologically self-obsessed. Self-obsession is different to arrogance. Being obsessed with how bad you are is quite torturous, but I'm not using pain to excuse myself here. The whole thing is hardly a virtue.

Getting up was hard. My bed was warm, the world was cold and grey. It was winter, but the weather wouldn't matter. I could've woken to a gorgeous blazing sun and narrowed my eyes, hissed and spat at it. I stumbled out of bed, straight to the bathroom. I would weigh myself three times: once left foot first, once right foot first, then left again – and always with a certain type of knickers. Sensible white ones. Girls in the changing rooms said I wore granny knickers. Those girls had knickers with cartoons on; some even wore thongs. We were thirteen.

I stepped onto the scales – feet not too far forwards –

oh, was that time a little wobbly? Best begin again. Got to be certain. Certainty. Not certain? Do it all again.

Sometimes Adam banged on the door: 'Can you *hurry up*? What the hell are you doing in there?'

'Fuck *off.*'

'I'm gonna be late for school!'

'Jessica, what's going on?' Mum's voice.

'Nothing.'

'Will you unlock this door please?'

'In a *minute!*'

Some time – a long time later – I would take my final reading. Not the last I would've liked, but I had to move on to my exercises. The scale said seven stone six.

'Seven and a half.'

'It's a little under.'

'Well, at least it isn't over. So that's OK.'

When exactly did the different voices enter my head? I did not remember. But one was strong, the other frightened, and the strong voice said I was OK that morning, so I was safe for the day.

Then the measuring of waist and hips – that took quite a while – then I hurried back to the bedroom for exercise. There was a buzzing in my brain, a strange high voice as hard as steel that kept me upright when I felt like falling down. I didn't know what it was called

31

but I knew that I needed it. It was making me survive, this voice, sure as a drip to the veins.

Exercise. Twenty lateral sit-ups either side to start with. '*That wasn't very good,*' the strong voice rebukes. '*Begin again.*' The voice is part of me and not part. I obey. Then I lose count, begin again. Then straight sit-ups, then waist exercises and so on. The strong voice said I must do them again – if I didn't go to the toilet first, if my underwear was in the wrong place, if I wasn't straight enough or too straight. It hurt. But I had to do it, because it kept me safe, and if I didn't, I knew that something terrible would happen. Eventually I had to leave for school. Whatever I had not completed to my satisfaction, I wrote on my hand for later.

School. God, I hated it. If it was bad before, now it was living hell. I had a kind of force field up around me, of crackling negative energy. Anger, hate, fear, warning people to keep away. Isolation is a cold place. I fidgeted through lessons, no idea what they were about, then sprinted home at lunch time to exercise again. After school I'd do more spots, then a fast 'dance session' to burn calories, more spots . . . then the spots again before I went to bed.

And food? The calorie book was like a Bible, never far from my hand; but I knew it almost by heart anyway,

32

it was just a comfort thing. I thought I was eating about 800 calories per day. I weighed and measured everything out on the kitchen scales, calculating again and again the percentage that came from fats. But I inflated the figure. How can you inflate printed figures? Well.

There is something funny about madness in the blackest sense of the word. For example: I was considering the calories on a yoghurt pot. I took the figure for calories per 100 grams and divided it by 100. God knows why. Just an inkling, I guess, that even the yoghurt manufacturers were lying to me. So I had the calories per gram. Then I multiplied that by the number of grams in a pot. The figure on my calculator read 98.3. But the yoghurt was only meant to be 98 calories! So I started counting the amount of calories as just a bit more than the figure on the packaging.

Then there was the ounce dispute. Some books claimed an ounce was 30 grams, some said 28. Which was correct? Our kitchen scales weighed in grams and nothing else. I worried that the kitchen scales thought an ounce was 30 grams, while the calorie book thought it was 28. So I was counting the calories for 30 grams of a product as though it were only 28! I devised a mathematical solution: if an apple was 11 calories per ounce, to be perfectly sure, I had to divide 11 by 28, then multiply it by 30. Then I multiplied *that* by the ounces it weighed, core included, and added a bit extra – to make sure. The apple came out about 90 calories. So when I counted out 800 a day, I guess the actual figure would be more like 400 or 300.

That's some serious maths. I hate maths, by the way. They used to think I was bad at it, because I could never be bothered. I would not have shown such ingenuity for anything less than slimness. But the disturbed mind is a powerful thing. 'Starvation heightens the faculties,' said Sherlock Holmes. That's true in the beginning – then it really screws them up. But at that time I was so high, I was flying. At school, I would sprint from class to class. At the same time I was utterly depressed. No surprise there – starvation *is* a depressive. Pole to pole and back again, just like a tennis ball. It was exhausting.

My family were concerned and confused:

'You're well skinny, Jess,' was Adam's verdict, and:

'You are now too thin,' my mum pronounced.

'No I'm not.' I looked at her like she was nuts.

'Where are you going now?'

'Down the shop.'

'Not till you've eaten something.'

'I have.'

'What?'

34

'An apple.'

'That isn't good enough. I want you to eat this cereal bar. Now.'

Mental check: 'I can't eat that! It's a hundred and forty-four calories!'

'If you don't eat this you're not going out.'

My jaw dropped: I was secretly thrilled. These were the sorts of threats made to people who actually *were* thin. Then joy was replaced by rage – what right did she have, what right?! This was my own life – I was building it myself, and I would order it. But Mum stood in front of the door. I could yell, or—

'Fine,' I said smoothly, and half smiled. 'I'll stay here.' High ground. I locked myself in my room, closed my eyes and relished the superior, clean feeling of emptiness inside my stomach.

I shut Rachel out. The poor girl tried:

'So you're going swimming, Jess? Can I come?'

'No,' I snapped. 'This is serious stuff.' If she came, she would slow me down. She'd want to stop and *talk to me* halfway through! I shuddered to think of it. Rachel kept phoning. I stopped answering the phone.

Even the cat didn't like me any more. Maybe he could see the force field crackle. But that was OK; I didn't like him either. I hated everything and everyone. Hated the days, hated the gnawing nights. The world was wicked, and the strong voice was my enduring lifeline in it.

People with eating disorders are experts at hiding food. I didn't bin it in the house – that would just be stupid – but I slipped things into pockets and disposed of them in the bin on the way to school. I smeared things on plates, knew how to leave the most flesh on an apple, hid food in handkerchiefs – there are a million small tricks. The feeling of control was quite a high. No one was in charge of me; I ate nothing that I didn't want to. This was my life, I could control it, and all the pain and suffering of the black world couldn't touch me. I only recall one instance when, almost automatically, I reached into the cupboard, got down a box of sugary cereal and started to stuff it into my mouth. Overcome with horror, I dashed to the bin and spat out all the soggy brown mess before I could swallow it. Scraped the crap out of my teeth.

I did not make myself sick; I wasn't crazy, after all.

My periods stopped. I'd started getting periods at eleven: heavy, dirty and disgusting things. I loathed them. I hated the look of dark blood coming out of my body. The worst was when it stained the bed sheets. Crimson-red on white. Disgusting. Dirty, dirty, dirty.

They made my tummy even fatter than it need be: that swelling betrayed my filthy female mechanisms, like letters branded on the forehead: WOMAN. My tummy should be flat, flat and innocent. And periods hurt! Who wanted them anyway? Not me.

'It's quite horrible,' Mum said experimentally, eyeing me for reaction, 'to think that when we diet, we don't give our bodies enough food, so their stores get used up. We've got to have energy. If we don't give our bodies enough food they break down our flesh for energy.'

I didn't think that was horrible. I thought it sounded cool. Hard. And I had to be hard. I had learned that already. Life is hard, and I had to be tough. So I would train my body to endure things, the way my mind could. I read about these Navy Seals once, who're trained to endure torture by detaching their minds from their bodies. They can lie there, having screws shoved under their thumbnails or God knows what – and just send their mind off somewhere else entirely. Ultimate endurance: it thrilled me. *I'd love to be able to do that!* I thought. *I'd love it!*

Mum took me to the GP about the periods and depression: a woman now, not the male doctor I'd seen as a younger child. The GP was not concerned. 'It's the speed of the weight loss,' she said, 'combined with the hormones. Besides, she *is* thirteen.' She half smiled at my mum as though this last proviso ought to explain it all. Then she had me step onto her great bar scales. They said I was seven eleven. *Eleven!* That was five pounds heavier than the scales at home.

'They're not very kind scales,' she said jokingly.

What the hell is she on about? I was enraged. *How can scales be kind or not kind? They're there to tell you the truth.*

'I know what you're thinking,' the GP said to Mum with a sideways look. 'I wouldn't worry about it. Nine out of ten teenage girls diet, and it only ever becomes a problem for something like one per cent.' No one had said the word yet. It's like a swear word. I'm hedging around it myself, even now.

ANOREXIA.

Most people are more willing to say 'fuck'. It's funny. Swearing, the taboo of my parents' generation, is fine now. So is sex and, mostly, homosexuality. But we don't talk about death any more, and anorexia is a killer. I reckon the decline of organized religion has something to do with this taboo on death. We don't like to talk about the end of this life because we're worried we're not banking up for what comes after it, if anything. Perhaps.

'Do you know about the Body Mass Index?' the GP asked both of us.

'No,' I said.

'Well, it's the scientific way of telling if people are over- or underweight. There's an equation using height and weight – you don't need to know it – and the answer is a number: a normal BMI is between nineteen and twenty-five. That's for adults, both men and women, and it's pretty generous. Right now, Jessica, your BMI is' – she pressed buttons on a calculator – 'twenty. I should say that's absolutely fine. Now I have some further questions . . .'

She began to ask about other things: my life, my school and my friends.

I thought, *Trivial, stupid, boring and depressing.* I answered, 'Fine.'

More questions – did I enjoy things I used to enjoy? Did I feel cut off from people? 'Yeah,' I had to admit. That was me all right. What could *she* do about it? A stab of anguished self-pity, which I instantly repressed.

'Well, I can tell you have some things you need to talk about,' she said fake-lightly at the end of our appointment. 'How would you like to meet with some-body experienced in this field?'

'Yeah, all right,' I replied, wondering what field she was talking about.

'Somebody' turned out to be a child psychologist, so alarm bells must have been ringing.

chapter five

December. I lived in a grey haze now, and it was getting darker. I could not stop fixating on the things I hated most: myself, and my masochistic daily rituals. I didn't really have fat left by that time, so since I was still starving I began to burn away my muscles as I exercised compulsively. You can feel it happening, even as you move. It hurts like nothing I have felt before or since. *But it's just as well for a girl to get pain into perspective,* I thought. *After all, we have the babies.*

'*Anyway,*' the hard voice said, '*you're a Navy Seal now.*' And I believed – believed I could detach my mind from my physical tortures – but the voice was lying. I lived in physical pain and mental torment. The amount I let myself eat went down and down. Necessary exercise went up. I continued to lose weight, but very slowly now, as my body fought to conserve the last of its reserves. I found reasons not to believe the scale. My appointment with the child psychologist was for 20 December, three weeks away. Three weeks can seem an awfully long time to somebody in such straits. I took to writing on my hands, on pieces of paper, tissues, anywhere: *Done 50 sit-ups this morning.*

But then I didn't believe it. *Wait – where was the second hand on the clock when I started? Must start again. Again.*

Then I thought of doing something bad. I didn't understand it at the time and I don't now, but the strong voice that kept me alive was a tyrant. I longed to escape from it. But how do you escape from what is part of you? I could see only one way out. I'd just returned from a manic run, I'd eaten almost nothing that day and my limbs were screaming. '*Enough,*' the scared voice begged. '*Enough.*' So I locked myself in the downstairs toilet with a bottle of bleach.

Standing in the room with its wallpaper of green ladies and parasols, I put my hand on the cap of the bottle. I wanted to die. I couldn't bring myself to slit my wrists – the very idea sickened me. I needed a more exotic, *abstract* way, like drinking poison. It somehow seemed a lot less awful. I had no poison, but I did have a bottle of bleach. I guessed if I drank enough, fast, it would kill me. Which is even crazier, because I bet it hurts a lot more and is generally more horrific than a couple of quick slashes.

I raised the bottle, wavered for a second. There genuinely was a fifty-fifty chance I'd chug it, but at the crunch I didn't. Maybe I was just too scared. Maybe I had a flash of sanity. Probably I was driven by survival instinct. Who knows – perhaps there was some outside force, set in stark opposition to the voice, that prevented me from drinking the bleach. I've had a pretty religious upbringing. And I do tend towards theism. Especially at night.

'I need help now!' I was standing in the living-room doorway, shouting. 'Not in two weeks!'

'I know, Jess, I'm sorry, but I can't make the appointment come any faster!'

'Why is it taking so long?'

'Because there are a lot of people out there who need help, and not a lot of doctors.'

'Don't patronize me! This isn't some normal fucking teenage crisis!'

'Jessica! I do not like that language!'

'Well it's true anyway! This is not normal! I am *not normal*!'

'Well I can't help you!' cried Mum. 'I don't know what's wrong with you!'

'Why not?'

'I don't know!'

'Why am I like this? What's happened to me to make me like this?'

'I don't know, Jess, I just don't know . . . Maybe you were born like it . . .'

'Oh, so it's my fault!'

'I didn't say that!' Her voice was breaking.

I could feel my eyes stretched, wildly: '*Nobody understands!*'

That was my constant cry throughout the winter. I burst into tears at school, during DT, a subject that I loathed. Mortified, I snivelled, 'I've got hay fever. It's nothing.'

'Funny, that,' said Joanne, a friend I'd forgotten, 'seeing as it's December.'

I ran out, resisting the impulse to stick my middle finger up at all of them: the grey-haired grey-faced teacher glanced up briefly from the shelter of his desk in mild surprise. The kids paused, then continued in their chaos.

I'm not the sort of person used to running out of lessons. My primary-school reports said 'model pupil'. I really love to learn. But anorexia brought out my nemesis Superbitch, and she didn't give a shit about school.

It all came to a head one Monday afternoon. Rain sluiced down appropriately in horizontal sheets, and I was attempting to sprint home, while juggling my school bag, my forsaken violin and a lattice mincemeat tart I'd baked in cookery. I'd added the calories and fat to my daily total – just in case I'd touched it, then touched my mouth. So I slipped and tripped and dropped it all, picked up the bag, the instrument and soggy lattice mess, and ran on in hysterics. Total strangers called to me, asked if I was all right. Oh God, the shame of it!

This was a pit, an inner darkness I did not know and had never guessed existed. Why were these things happening to me? Devils were dancing on my shoulders. I slammed the door behind me, crying, rain-soaked, and I poured out the story to my mother. Why was I crying? I was not a crying girl. I was too hard, too unbreakable for that weak mush. But I was breaking. My body and my mind were giving in. I hope that people only go there, down that pit, once in their lifetime, maximum. I hope you get immunity to it, like measles.

'You're physically and mentally exhausted,' she said frantically, because the a-word is taboo. 'Come on. You're going to bed now.'

'I can't!' I shrieked. 'I have to do my exercises!'

She grabbed my arm and dragged me. I resisted each

step of the way to my room but my reserves were giving out. I did not have the strength to pull back any more.

'Let me go, let me go!' I wailed.

'Look at you!' Mum shouted as she pulled my clothes over my head, like a little girl. 'You look like a skeleton.'

I can't remember what I weighed at that point, but I do remember how my ribs protruded through the fabric of the nightgown. She made me get into bed. Now I was seething. It was debasing, and I'm proud. All my attempts at being strong, at being adult and unbreakable, had come to this: the dignity of a baby or less. At least babies have a reason for being like that – I was just stupid and weak. And then she broke it, broke the secret rule:

'Do you know what you have?'

'No . . .'

'You have *anorexia*, Jessica!' And then she called the doctor.

Prince William was on the television. I had a little telly in my room, but it had not been on for months. No time for that. The prince was on a foreign tour. Little African children with painted faces danced about in a schoolhouse and he laughed and played with them. I'd sort of forgotten there was such a place as Africa. A hot, faraway place where the earth is burned and people are *grateful* for whatever food they can get. Alien. Mum let me do my evening exercises, because I begged, but I was oddly pierced with disappointment as I did them.

Later, I heard Adam come in and creep upstairs, very quietly. He shut himself in his room.

The GP came in the morning and diagnosed me with depression. She gave me little white tablets called Prozac. I'd never heard of it before: she didn't explain much, just that they were designed to lift people's mood; she warned me they would take some time to work. When she left I went and ran across the park ten times.

'Don't go,' Mum begged, catching my wrist as I made to go out of the door.

I very calmly took her hand, removed it from my arm and met her eyes with a look that said, *Back off*. The voice said that running would keep me together for just that little bit longer, so run I would. She watched me go, helpless – watched still as I came home afterwards, sat down, then got up and went back to the park to do two lengths to make sure I really had done ten. It was still raining like hell.

chapter six

The twentieth of December came, eventually. A Wednesday; I huddled in the front seat of the car, hiding in my black coat and hat, head down.

The psychologist's appointment was at a clinic on the other side of town. On the outside, it looked like an imposing old grey mansion. But walking in, we were assailed by bright colours and childish murals, paintings of children holding hands. We went through into a waiting room, where magazines and plastic toys lay in heaps. The walls were grey and dull beneath the pictures; you could see the pipes with their lagging. I saw a boy, my age or not much younger, wearing something like the blue pyjamas I had been dressed in as a child. It felt weird not to be in school. Now I knew I really was different.

The child psychologist was called Dr James. To my surprise, she was a woman. She was also pretty and quite young, with long fair hair, bright green eyes and a kind, pink smile. I liked her instantly.

Her office resembled a classroom but with fewer chairs. Large airy windows looked down onto the lawn. Shafts of wintry sunlight fell in rectangles on the floor. On the walls were more childish paintings. There was a desk, too, but she didn't sit behind it. She sat facing us in a little ring, open-postured, smiling. Psychiatric tactics, but she did them well, and I'll grudgingly concede I needed them.

'You must be Jessica, and Jessica's mum.' Dr James was speaking softly, with an Irish accent. 'My name is Sarah.'

I nodded, wary, force field up against a challenge, at the same time wanting to spill. Was I going to tell all? It was almost tempting: at least I would be taken seriously. Sarah began to question me in a general way: about my life, my school, my friends. Then:

'How much do you weigh?' Dr James was looking at me, and I saw then that beneath the kind, compassionate smile was a needle-sharp perception, hard layers of resilience. Her eyes reminded me of calm green waters concealing deposits of rock.

'Seven and a half stone.' I believed it.

'To me, Jessica, you look more like seven, maximum. And there is no doubt in my mind you have an illness.'

'Yes . . .' I waited, glancing briefly at my mother.

'The name of that illness is anorexia nervosa.'

Silence. So someone with a PhD had said it at last, that forbidden phrase. You could almost hear the thunder in the distance. My mum had said it, but that didn't count: she'd also told me I was beautiful. To hear 'anorexia nervosa' on the lips of this clever, grave, compassionate young woman made it real. So real. I was terrified. I was startled. Then I was filled with glee. That strong voice, that weird part of me, turned somersaults of delight. *Well done, Jess, well done!* Now I was really special, really troubled. No one could ignore my pain, or dismiss it as a piece of teenage moodiness any longer.

'There are four criteria for anorexia,' continued Dr James. 'You meet them. The first is maintaining a body weight fifteen per cent below normal, which I can tell by looking at you that you are doing. The second is intense fear of fatness or weight gain, which your mother has described to me. The third is a distorted body image, which you clearly have, and the fourth is the absence of at least three periods in a row, in female sufferers.'

'So I'm sort of a textbook case then?' I asked wonderingly. This was incredible. She might as well have announced: *Jessica, you are the empress of a long-neglected galaxy.* To a fat person, which I had been, the Anorexic is a near-mythical figure. The glamorous heights of her thoughts can't be guessed at. What was an anorexic like? I'd often wondered. But now *I* was anorexic. I, my own self, part of the definition. It boggled the mind. Unbelievable.

'Well, if you looked up anorexia in a textbook you would certainly find a lot of information that describes you.' And I'd thought I was unique. 'The first thing that I want to do' – she had out the pens and paper, coloured and chunky – 'is set down some ground rules.'

I agreed. I sort of wanted rules by then, because things were getting so crazy. I resolved that I would listen and accept them.

'Number one: getting rid of the kitchen scales.'

Resolve went out of the window. The scales! You wouldn't yank the tube out of an IV drip. I looked at her like she was crazy.

'Number two: you must have a thousand calories a day, as counted by your mum. The idea is to slow down your weight loss.'

I couldn't have 1,000 calories a day. I'd just balloon. But they wouldn't understand that, so more urgently I demanded: 'How can she count out calories without scales?' Ha. Let them answer that one with their crazy rules!

'I can estimate, Jessica,' said Mum.

'But you won't get it right!' How could she? Nobody understood how to do these things right except me!

'Yes I will. I watched my weight for years without scales.'

The rest of the rules were a blur, but we cried on the way home.

'People die of it,' said Mum. 'People die.'

chapter seven

Dr James said that I was a 'deeply entrenched anorexic'. Entrenched is quite a good word for the suffocating mesh of rules and fear-driven compulsions.

The media tries to pass off anorexia as some teenage angsty drama, fuelled by photographs of thin celebrities and peer-group pressure to be skinny. *Noooooooo.* Anorexia's not about fashion. Hollywood imagery isn't the cause. Not that I'm saying those pictures help: obviously holding thinness up as success, beauty and achievement *can* add fuel to the perfectionist's fire. But many anorexics hate that phoney stuff, because they hate the world. The thinness is an outer manifestation of a deep inner problem. As for being thin to feel better about yourself, forget it.

Anorexia is about fear and guilt and obsession and the drive for absolute perfection. It's about the loss of innocence and childhood. Bereavement, divorce and fractured families are the pressing factors, not glossy magazines. Practically all teenagers diet. But madness is a whole different ball game.

The night after my appointment there was the school Christmas concert. Strange – it was Christmas. I was playing the violin in the orchestra, as I had done every other year of my life since I was seven. It was like a tradition. I was never an amazing violinist, but I was competent, when I made time to practise. And I always liked to play in orchestras. There's a sense of unity to it. Of contributing your strands of music to a good cumulative sound. That year it was awful. Before Mum would let me get changed into my uniform, she presented me with a terrifying sandwich. It contained a poached egg, some ham and some salad. *It's probably swimming with butter!* Frantically I tried to add up the calories in my head, and came up with some inflated total in the hundreds.

'Why are you doing this to me?' It came out as almost a scream.

'Because I love you,' said my mum.

I gagged on every crumb.

At the concert I did not play well. All right, I played terribly. I put two F naturals in the key of D major. I have known since I was eight that there are no F naturals in that key. I could barely hold my bow correctly;

I could feel that sandwich in my stomach like a rock the whole way through 'The Holly and the Ivy', 'O Little Town of Bethlehem' and the rest.

The parents sat in the main part of the hall, on crappy plastic chairs because there weren't enough of the good kind to go round. The orchestra played at the back, beneath the massive carved cross (Jesus as an abstract figure, smiling and fully clothed while being crucified). Every year we wrapped strands of tinsel round the pegs of our violins and violas, or whatever part of a flute you can wrap tinsel round without spoiling the sound. When the choir came on to sing, they filed out in front of us.

The final number of the concert was always, *always* 'Once in Royal', with the choir and the orchestra and everyone. Strings draw the final notes out, brass give it all, the audience are forced to stand and sing. Plaid-jumpered fathers grumbled out the melody over beer-bellies, lipsticked mothers balanced fraying smiles. I had always looked out for my mother, because I used to feel proud of how she sat without my dad, while other people's parents came pre-packed as sets of two. This year I felt nothing for her.

The hall was hot, from all the crowded bodies and the falsity, but I was cold that year. I felt fat and disgusting. Other years I didn't mind the fakeness of the concert, because it was cheerful-fake at least, but that year I just left as fast as I could possibly pack my violin, before the mince pies came around. I was supposed to eat some more when I got home, some supper, but I just picked at it. We were supposed to write down everything I ate or didn't eat in a little notebook for Dr James. The first day went down as a failure.

chapter eight

Did I think I was still fat?

Well, sometimes. I could look in the mirror and see bloated fatness, especially my tummy. I know I saw myself as bigger than I was, because a week before Christmas my mother dragged me shopping.

'Would you like those?' She pointed to a pair of trousers, size eight. I looked at them and snorted. 'You must be joking. Those trousers are for people like Katie Albright.'

Katie Albright was the canon of thinness. She had been in my class throughout primary school. She was and always had been as tall and thin as a willow-wand, with tiny shoulders and hips. Her mother said she didn't eat well: but she certainly ate chocolate, and crisps, and seemingly whatever else she wanted, and never gained an ounce of fat. She just grew taller and stayed skinny. Now, in Year Nine, she still had no hips and no breasts to speak of. Nobody envied her much, except me: lucky

Katie, permitted to eat anything she wanted, by being as thin as that!

'Trust me, these will fit you,' said my mum. And they did.

'But they look different now,' I brushed it off. 'They look much bigger on me than they did on the hanger.'

Other days, or even other times of day, I would think I looked all right now. But there was no way I could eat a single calorie more than Mum forced down me, no way I could ease up on my exercise, because I'd put weight on. And every time the scales went down a pound, that would become the new weight that I couldn't go above. I don't know what I thought would happen if I did, save that it would be very, very bad, and the thought of it filled me with terror.

Such fear is hard to describe. And it's so *stupid* – sandwiches aren't frightening: murderers and tsunamis are frightening. Kitchen scales aren't essential to live: air is essential to live. But that fear is real. Imagine being locked inside a dark room with a million spiders crawling up your arms, down your legs, into your hair. That is how my omnipresent terror felt. When people are that scared, they're horrible. They're also sort of pathetic.

* * *

It all went to hell the next day. I was in the middle of another obsessive exercising session in my bedroom. Suddenly my muscles clenched and burning pains shot through me. I fell to the floor with a thud and burst into tears.

'Jessica!' My mum came in so fast I knew she had been listening outside the door. 'What's going on?'

'I can't, I can't, but I have to!' I wailed.

'You can't because you're starving!'

I had refused most of my breakfast, begging, 'I can't, I can't, I'll be sick,' and at last Mum had given in before my tears and anger. Now she disappeared and returned with a cereal bar.

'Eat this.'

'No!' Panic.

'If you eat that you'll be massive,' snarled the awful voice, and I crushed down my body's hunger – it was more urgent to placate my mind. *'Massive, huge, look at it, stuffed with fat and calories . . .'* Now the bar looked revolting, poisonous, and my stomach recoiled at the thought. I clamped shut my lips.

My mother got down on the floor and looked at me for a long moment. 'Jessica,' she said deliberately, 'why can't you?' Fear was in her face. I could feel my eyes

stretched wide in an expression that must have carica-
tured madness.

'Because,' I rasped, 'there is a voice. A voice inside
my head.'

'What kind of voice?'

'A strong one.'

'I think the voice is evil.'

'Yes' – I nodded frantically – 'it's evil. But I need it.'
How could I explain? I hated it and I clung to it. It was
killing me, but it was keeping me alive. It was so loud,
so constant, so strong in control now . . . without it, I'd
crumble to dust. *But I'm already crumbling* – a faint, tired
whisper. I spread my hands. 'I need it.'

'I'm phoning Dr James,' she said, and got up. My
mind forced new energy into my limbs; I followed to
the top of the stairs.

'Yes . . . yes . . .' my mum was saying, and scrawling
things on a pad. I waited, heart beating, fingernails
gouging the banister.

'Get your coat,' said Mum when she hung up.

'Where are we going?'

'A clinic. You're going to see some different
doctors.'

'You mean like a loony bin?'

She turned and looked at me. 'It's called an

adolescent psychiatric unit, Jessica. It's where you need to be.'

In the car I considered it. The madhouse, the loony bin. A place out of distant legend. Nobody I knew had ever been in one – I hadn't even known there *was* one in the city. And suddenly, desperately, I wanted to be in this unit. I wanted to be in a place where people would protect me from the monstrous voice, where I would have a reason, a legitimate excuse not to exercise, because if I was in hospital, obviously I was sick. Whereas if I was outside, and ordinary, there was no excuse. It all seemed perfectly logical. The fact that in the unit I would be forced to eat, which I'd refused to do at home, simply did not occur to me. Now I built the unit up into a kind of sanctuary – this would be my salvation. It just had to be.

The unit wasn't hard to find: a small building next to the main hospital. If the previous clinic had looked like a primary school, this place was more like a nursery. *I'm regressing.* I was wrapped up once more in my black coat with my hat pulled down so that it almost covered my eyes. We went in through a set of glass doors and stood in reception.

'Jessica has an appointment to see Doctor Jane Wright

at eleven thirty,' my mum told the woman. A funny feeling had come over me – like my tongue was all stuck to the roof of my mouth. I don't think I could have spoken my own name if I'd had to, let alone what I was doing there. It was a strange place, with a disinfectant smell.

While we waited, I clenched in my stomach. It was a technique that the voice called '*posturing*'. I'd picked up the term from my piano teacher, who was fabulously fit and slim. Posture is important when you play an instrument, and she'd mentioned at some time that it also gave your stomach muscles good tone. I wasn't sure how often or how long I had to hold it: so to be on the safe side, I did it all the time. All day long I went round with my stomach clenched in a painful way. So I could never actually relax, whether sitting, standing or lying down. My mind was always buzzing with fear. *Am I doing it right? Is it working?* Madness is so tiring. It wears the brain away.

After a while a tall, austere woman with steely grey hair cropped short around her head came into the lobby. Hard, intelligent grey eyes drank me in from behind wire-rimmed glasses. I knew straight away that this was Wright. She looked like a doctor, or perhaps a lawyer. The prosecution. Most important of all, she was *thin*: *That's not fair! How come she's allowed to be that thin and I'm not? Bloody hypocrite.* I loathed her on sight.

She led us to a small office. Desk, chairs and shutters on the windows. It was a freezing winter's day, but you couldn't have seen the sun in there if it had been June. A whiteboard was up on the wall for some reason. A small, dumpy woman with mouse-brown hair and a pleasant face was seated in a chair. She had nice eyes, rather like a hamster I once owned. Her name, said Wright, was Julie Peterson, and she was a dietician. *Then why's she fat?* I demanded mentally. I didn't give people a break.

There were other people there, including a large and rather baffled-looking man with thin sandy hair. His name was Fred, and he turned out be the most senior of the lot: I think his title was Consultant Psychiatrist. He carried a Fireman Sam lunchbox in his big hand. Everywhere.

I sat in one of the chairs, and peered out at them all from under the brim of my hat. I felt a sudden desperation. OK, so this was what I needed. All these clever, high, official-looking people were set to take away the monster that at first had been my ally but had now become my tormenter. I wanted to hand it straight over, that moment. I honestly truly did.

'I want to be in here,' I said.

'We can't admit you immediately, Jessica,' Wright said,

looking sharply at me. 'Almost everybody is on Christmas leave. But once the patients return, we will not have a spare bed.'

'But I can't cope at home!' I wailed. 'Don't take me home again, Mum, I'm going to die there.' I later learned that this was a first. Everybody else fights tooth and nail to avoid admission to the unit. As I'm told, I just gotta be different. To me, it was suddenly a magic wand; salvation had been offered on a golden platter – now it was being whisked away again, right from under my nose.

'You're not going to die.' Mum put her arm around me. 'Whatever happens, you're not going to die. Could she be admitted – to some sort of general hospital?'

Dr Wright frowned and opposed it. 'You could wreak havoc on a children's ward, Jessica,' she told me. She used my name in every sentence, even though we'd met about six minutes earlier. I don't know if it was meant to sound nice, personal, but it just sounded patronizing. Who the hell else was she talking to?

'*Oh*, they'd say, *another anorexic*. They'd let you run off to the shower, Jessica, and do your exercises – nobody would stop you. But if you hang on a while, Jessica, you'll come here, where you will be treated like an individual.'

'I can't,' I groaned, and dissolved into tears. The second time in one day.

Dr Wright said nothing for a moment. 'Is there some relative you could stay with for a while?' she asked my mother. 'Just for the change of scene?'

'How about going to London to stay with your uncle?' Mum asked me.

'No, no! It won't work. I need to be here.' Strange looks were passed between the high professionals. This plea was new to them.

'You *will* be here, Jessica,' they told me. 'Just not yet.'

Then they took me off to be weighed and measured. We passed through the lobby area again and took the right-hand door, then on down a short passage with many doors. The walls were vaguely pink, but sickly pale pink. And I encountered the smell for the first time: the unit smell. It wasn't good or bad then, just strong and distinctive, but it came to be the worst smell in the world to me. Later the air would seem thick with it. It made you gag. Every time you breathed, its fingers clawed your throat like a bulimic.

Coming out of one of the doors was a little girl. I thought she was about twelve years old, and extremely pretty. She had elfin features and this lovely white skin – no trace of blemishes or pimples. Her eyes were clear green. She was very small, in height, in weight, in every way. Her hands were like a doll's. She smiled at me sweetly, very small and shy. But knowing. Sad and knowing. Then I understood: she wasn't twelve.

By the time it registered with me to smile back, she'd gone.

We went on into the room. The nurse told me to strip down to my tights and T-shirt. It was bloody freezing in that room. And so small and dingy. I'd heard about the NHS being poor before, but I'd imagined hospitals of any sort as bright, white buildings with pristine tiled floors and airy windows. Not that I'd ever been in hospital before. I was a really healthy child.

I can't remember what I weighed then – the numbers don't matter any more – but obviously I was under-weight, though these scales weighed heavier than the ones at home. The thing to measure height was broken.

Back in the office, my mother and the dietician wrote me out a meal plan of 1,000 calories a day, designed to slow down my weight loss. I saw it and sobbed again. Impossible. It wouldn't work, it couldn't. I left the unit crying my eyes out. I wanted to stay and be helped. Strange things were happening to me physically. I could cling to radiators till my skin was red and still be cold inside. A fine coat of soft brown hair had begun to creep over my stomach, back and chest: the body's last-ditch attempt to keep warm. There was a permanently sick taste in my throat and mouth: the burning of body tissue. And I couldn't stop, could not stop. I was in terror of breaking the rituals. Prozac was doing nothing. The strong voice drove me on, pushed harder. I obeyed it.

The next day was Saturday, 23 December. I was scared to be alone at night. We moved my bedclothes into the granny flat where my nan used to live when she was with us, and my mum brought hers in too.

'We'll sleep here for now,' she said.

I tried to carry on as normal with the exercises, but I was crying with desperation as I did them. Every movement hurt but I could not stop. There seemed no way out. Funnily, my thoughts of suicide did not return, at least not then, because I was never alone. At last my mother called the GP back and she stood over me, watching as I struggled through my sit-ups.

'I don't understand it!' cried my mother. 'Physically, how can she be doing this? On what she's eating?'

'I agree that she should not be able to. But she's still finding resources, from somewhere.'

They sedated me. That brought relief. I was able to just stop: more because I had a reason, an excuse, than because I was physically incapable. So in the evening I got into bed. I waited. I don't know what for. Time slowed.

Everything had stopped.

My brain had stopped.

Perhaps the world was ending.

Mine was, at least.

Then something happened: the GP called the unit, and a man called a consultant came to speak about admittance as a day patient. I don't remember what he said, except that at the end I wanted to get up and exercise again.

'You've waited a long time for this medication, Jessica,' he said to me. 'Why don't you let it work?'

So I did.

That must be amongst the strangest conversations I have had in my whole life. During the next days, under sedation, I couldn't even wash myself any more. My mother had to do it. I was thirteen. I stopped eating altogether, because I wasn't exercising. I drank some HighLights once a day and other liquids. Nothing poisonous like milk or juice of course. Visitors kept coming from the unit but I don't remember them. I remember some things about Christmas, though, for the Monday was Christmas Day.

That day I ate some vegetables from a tiny bowl. They felt like rocks, forcing themselves down my oesophagus, hard and boulder-heavy in my stomach. I lost about a pound a day, because my body had shut down. That is the strangest feeling. It's like nothing else I've ever felt. Almost like watching yourself down a telescope, or at the end of a long dark tunnel, floating apart from your body. I was never hungry, except before I fell asleep. Then a little whining part of me appealed to the hard part:

'Can't I have something to eat? I'm hungry now.'

'Of course not. You already brushed your teeth,' it answered. *'God knows how many calories were in that.'*

My mum came in to kiss me goodnight. I feebly pushed her away: 'Don't kiss me.'

'Why not?'

'Because . . . because you were drinking tea and maybe . . . . maybe, the tea will be on your lips . . . and it will go on my skin and . . .'

'What? You'll absorb calories?'

'Maybe.'

Oh, my brain was too confused. I went to sleep.

Sometimes my mother read to me. I was reading *Great Expectations*. It remains a favourite story of mine, yet I will never be completely comfortable with it. To this day, Mr Pip and Mr Pocket cannot fail to conjure up images of that dark flat, of the fire, of the deadening, numbing tiredness.

I did not see Adam once at Christmas, nor did I think about him.

On Boxing Day I made myself get up. Someone from the unit called and said I'd have a bed there on the 27th – but I couldn't think that far ahead. I started walking around the house and using cans as weights. My mum told me a long time afterwards that even when I was at my most horrible, most vicious, her overwhelming feeling for me was pity.

PART TWO:
RAGING

chapter one

As much as I loathed Jane Wright, it was she who first described the illness as a monkey. 'A monkey on your shoulder' was her phrase. I don't know if she coined it, but it certainly is apt. It doesn't describe the whole thing, obviously; but it's a damn good analogy for the insidious, influential voice that pops up in the head. So the new name for the bad voice was the Monkey; and a devilish-looking, skeletal one she was.

Here's the really strange thing: she wasn't my first Monkey. It wasn't even the first time I'd heard the phrase. I'd been using 'Monkey' to myself for years. I first saw it in a book I read when I was eleven. *Misery*, by Stephen King.

I don't know if I should've been reading that stuff at eleven, but you couldn't stop me. I taught myself to read when I was about three, and I haven't really stopped since. They used to do these tests in primary school to find your reading age. By first year juniors I was off the scale. I was not the best at science, and my maths was scraping average. I could've been better, they said, but I didn't care enough. I just cared for stories. That's an understatement. I am passionate about them. Need them like food and water. *As long as there are books around,* I used to think, *I'm happy.* By the time I was ten, children's stories weren't cutting the mustard, except the wonderful, amazing ones such as *The Animals of Farthing Wood.* The kind you love for ever, even after you're grown up. I had all the *Farthing Wood* books: *The Siege of White Deer Park* and *In the Grip of Winter,* all those later ones with better titles but without the inspiration of the first.

So by the time I was eleven, you couldn't stop me reading *Misery.*

The Monkey sentence comes from a man who is taking drugs. Originally, they're for pain after the accident he's had, but it gets to the point where he knows he isn't really taking these drugs for the pain any more, he's taking them for 'the monkey downstairs'. Well, even at eleven I knew I had a monkey downstairs. I didn't verbalize it, but the Monkey became my name for the darker, secret part of me. On the outside, my outer level, which is thankfully the practical part, things like blood and anguish and violence and most especially war are scary and repulsive. But the Monkey likes them.

The Monkey is the dark part that relishes that sort of stuff and hankers after it, a curiosity that borders on fascination. Even from my youngest years, from four or five, I thought about that sort of stuff in my bed late at night, and I liked it. When I got older it was almost sexual. I don't know why I thought I was unique in this: why do we have programmes like *Casualty* and *ER* that are so successful, if I am the only person ever to be fascinated by a bit of blood and anguish? Why are there disaster movies, war films, or psychological thrillers? Why did *Misery* ever get published? Because people like that stuff. Yet no one ever talks about those thoughts. So I felt freakish and unique and just a little special.

But now the Monkey was something else. It was anorexia. And for the first time I could verbalize it. It was almost a relief to use the word. The Monkey. Of course she's part of me, the darkest bleakest part, but when it's got a name it's almost easier to fight it.

chapter two

'I've changed my mind.' It was the day of my admittance, and I was being dressed before the fire in the flat. The only place I could bear to be stripped off. 'I don't want to go in.'

'You have to.'

'I want to weigh myself. I haven't weighed myself in days. I must have put on loads, lying around like this.'

'But you've hardly eaten anything!' I looked at my mum in confusion. What was she talking about? Remember that Slim-a-Soup yesterday? Besides which, that wasn't the point – everyone knew lazing around made you fat.

'You don't understand,' I grated.

'Well, you're not weighing yourself.'

'Yes. I. Am.'

'No you're not! I'm your mother!'

I steeled myself and walked towards the doorway. She moved to stop me.

'*I'm going!*' I shrieked suddenly, in pure rage, and she started back in shock. In the end she let me. Six stone six on the heavier scales. Fear and joy.

When we got to the unit that morning, the promised bed was not available, so I was admitted as an outpatient. Admission was a series of flurried meetings, some papers signed, a visit to a doctor in another freezing clinic room. I was holding in my stomach so tight I couldn't breathe. I remember people telling me, over and over, that it would not do any good. They were all against me – obviously on the side of this bad thing that was just waiting to spring out at me if I let go. Trust only the Monkey, for that is sure.

The next thing I remember clearly is sitting in the unit 'library' with my mother and two nurses. When I first heard I was going to the library I was happy. Libraries have always been my havens. But it turned out to be just another sick-pink room with chairs, a table and big windows. There wasn't a book in the place! Not even a shelf or a case where they once might have been. What liars these people were, what outright liars. If I had seen one book in what they called a library it would have made me happier. '*Why are you surprised?*' the Monkey asked. '*Libraries are good places. There's nothing good for you here.*'

One nurse was a man called Clive, quite old, with a kind, wrinkly face and a soft voice. The woman was called Eleanor. She looked just like a troll. She really did. She had squinty, staring, bulbous eyes and skin like leather. Dyed orange hair and a nose all bent over to the side. Her lips were pursed up with distaste as she looked at me. Trembling inside, I returned her gaze like flint. Anger made me sit up straight. My faculties suddenly clicked back into action. I was trapped within a ring of enemies conspiring to make me get fat. Well, they could not make me. I would stay small, I would stay thin, where I was safe. I squared my shoulders and glared.

'The first thing we'll do is give her lunch,' they were saying. 'She isn't thinking clearly from lack of food.'

Will you fuck, I thought, my tenuous hold on reality loosening a little bit further. *I'm thinking clearly all right. And I'm thinking I won't stay in this place for a second longer than I have to.*

Eleanor went out to phone the kitchens in the main part of the hospital. She returned and put to me a choice of tuna pasta or roast lamb. I opted for the tuna as it's lower calorie; as it happens, I hate lamb anyway, but if it had been less fattening I would have picked it.

My mum went away – I think to sign more papers

and be told about the treatment at the clinic. Eleanor went with her, thankfully. If I had a force field, so did she. She moved like she was striding into battle. Clive, the other nurse, took me through into the dining room. There were no other patients there at that time; as Wright had told me, they were home for Christmas. The dining room looked like a cross between a school canteen and a committee meeting room. An oblong plastic table ran the length of it, with one of those long hatch-openings at the far end with hot metal plates that they serve you the food from at school. A door beside it led into the kitchens.

I sat down on one side of the table. Clive and a young blonde girl-nurse sat across from me. They spoke pleasantly and cheerfully, like we were new friends just meeting in the yard or something. The blonde girl went behind the bar and there was a clattering of steel trays. Then a plate of pasta was set down before me. It was in a tomatoey sauce, with some kidney beans and bits of processed veg, and a synthetic cheesy topping, which I instantly peeled aside. It looked and smelled like cat sick, and the tuna was AWOL. Ah, the joys of a hospital menu.

The blonde girl was still smiling and talking to me as I pushed the goop around on my plate. I felt patronized and angry, but kept civil; until the Clive-man asked me what Santa had brought me for Christmas. What the hell was that supposed to mean? One, I was thirteen and highly intelligent, and two, I was disturbed, according to them. I had not had a happy clappy Christmas. Clive raised his eyebrows in blithe expectation of a response.

'Let me think,' I answered acidly: 'Prozac.'

What a bitch. But they didn't seem at all perturbed. I think the girl was laughing. I continued to dissect my meal. A few little pieces of chopped veg went down. Then three or four pieces of pasta. They didn't appear to be watching me so closely; Clive was studying the wall behind my head with a bland, placid look in his eyes. I arranged the rest in an artistic mural, mostly heaped around the edges of the plate.

'I'm done,' I said politely.

'You haven't eaten that,' said Clive. 'You've picked at it and eaten mostly vegetables.'

Bloody hell, I thought, *he's brighter than he looks!* It did not occur to me that I was merely the latest in a long and cunning line of anorexics, many of them more devious and practised than I. Nor that Clive here did have psychiatric training, and at least a few years' experience under his belt. That's the self-absorption of the illness for you, and the fear.

Textbook case or not, you still imagine you're the only one to do it. Ever.

Next I ate the sweetcorn; higher calorie than most veg, but vegetable nonetheless. Clive was having none of it.

'All of it,' he said.

I didn't have the guts to fling it in his face, so in the end I ate most of the pasta, all of the veg and a tiny scraping of the cheese. The Monkey was screaming and raging. My face was stone.

'All right, we'll let you get away with that for now,' said Clive.

'Get away with what?' I asked, incredulous. So far as the Monkey was concerned, I'd had a banquet.

chapter three

After lunch a nurse led me into the 'TV room'. I had no
word or sight of my mum. The room was small and grey-
walled with a window opening onto the yard; less homely
than the name would have you guess, but it did at least
have a television. Also a beaten-up couch, a straight-backed
chair and a beanbag. I sat up in the chair and held my
stomach in. The blonde nurse was still with me, and after
a while an older woman relieved her. I didn't know it,
but I was on 'levels': one of the higher rates of supervi-
sion. It means one nurse has to be with the patient at all
times. It's used for people they consider it dangerous to
leave alone, but who are not expected to be violent or
need physical restraint. The degree can go right up to
three-on-one. I've even heard of five. That day, I don't
actually think 'levels' was really necessary for me: I wasn't
in the mood for suicide, I was wary and alert and frightened like an animal, and in the mood to survive.

'Would you like to watch a video?' the nurse asked me.

'OK.' She put on Disney's *The Aristocats*, but the all-singing, all-dancing moggy ensemble only blurred before my eyes. I felt cold and sad and scared, and I did not believe them when they told me that 'holding my posture' wasn't doing anything for the muscles.

In the middle of the afternoon a girl a few years older than me came in and threw herself down on the sofa. She had pretty eyes, a rounded, friendly face with some spots, and a girlish dimple appeared when she smiled. The nurse looked over and smiled.

'Hi,' said the girl.

'Hello.'

'I'm Bethany.'

'My name is Jessica.'

'You're gonna be a day patient here, are you?'

'Yeah. I s'pose so.'

'Cool.'

So I had met another crazy teenager. She certainly didn't sound it. She wasn't anorexic either, because she wasn't thin enough. The only clue that something could be wrong was a slightly subdued manner; a weariness, if you like. An almost old look in her lovely eyes, as though very little she could see now would surprise her. I could not imagine what she might have done to get here, and I didn't ask. Instead, I kept sneaking little sideways glances at her, searching for some clue. Bethany lay back and closed her eyes as though the day had worn her out already.

Unfazed, the Aristocats sang on.

Presently we heard footsteps outside in the corridor. A nurse put her head round the door and asked me to come for a medical. Back to the cold clinic room; a doctor had come over from the main part of the hospital. A white coat, stethoscope and all. The notion that I hadn't held my stomach in for quite some time hit me like a bolt of thunder.

'You lazy bitch!' the Monkey shrieked.

Anguished, I quizzed the doctor: 'I want to tone my stomach muscles,' I explained to him. 'Will it help if I have a good posture?'

'You can't improve your muscles at the moment,' he answered. 'Without food, you can only erode them further.'

'But posture . . .' I insisted. 'Isn't it good?'

He paused, puzzled, then conceded: 'Well, it's always good to sit up straight, yes.'

Ha! So he was a liar too! He'd just said I couldn't do anything to tone the muscles, then he'd said I ought to! *'You can't trust anyone in this place,'* advised the Monkey. *'Better go with my ideas, kid. At least I'm consistent.'*

The doctor took my blood pressure and did some

other things with gadgets, then gave the physical diagnosis: 'You need to put some weight on.'

Like hell, I thought.

Then they called me back into the dining room for tea, served by a nursing assistant. She didn't question my choice of a plain jacket potato, and didn't even make me eat much of it. I was surprised – and pleased. *The fact is, she has no idea who I am or what I'm doing here.*

After several minutes Bethany came into the hall and sat opposite me at the table, chatting idly and pleasantly to the assistant. Just as I was finishing, she rolled up her sleeves and placed her elbows on the tabletop. My breath caught in my throat.

I had heard about self-harm before – self-mutilation – but never met or talked to anyone who had actually done it. Bethany's wrists and arms were covered – *covered* – with knife and razor slashes, crisscrossing, overlapping, zigzagging every way. Some were old purple scars and some were new, some light scratching like a child makes on a surface with a pencil, some the deep and vicious gouges of pure desperate loathing rage. *But – but*, I stammered in my mind, *but she's so nice! What would make her? Why would she want to do that to herself?*

Her old and lovely eyes regarded me across the tabletop. I looked down at my lap.

chapter four

I went home in the evening.

'How was it?' asked Adam, hovering in the doorway nervously.

'Great,' I said flatly, and went upstairs. To bed. My emotions were on shut-down, I was in a total daze. But after a sedative I slept, long and deep. Relief, maybe, that the exercise-circle was broken. But I had to do something about the food. I could not keep eating like they made me. I felt bloated, my stomach like an overblown balloon: pasta *and* two bites of baked potato that day, and I hadn't worked it off! *Lazy – fat bitch – ought to move now* . . . I thought drowsily as I drifted into sleep. But the sedatives worked in proportion to body weight. I was out like a light within minutes.

Early in the morning my mother drove me back to the unit. We didn't talk in the car, but she hugged and kissed me emphatically before leaving. I was pleased but slightly unnerved by the unaccustomed contact.

'Be good,' she said, and the word now held strange contradictions. *Good* was supposed to mean eating little, getting slim. All I'd ever been trying to do was be good.

The first thing I did was ask every person on duty if my muscles were ready to tone yet. After all, I'd eaten lunch and some tea the previous day. Got to use those calories for something.

'Jessica,' said a nurse wearily, 'you need more calories than that just to live. Your heart has to keep beating and your blood pumping. Your body is still breaking down its muscles and the last strains of fat.'

On an intellectual level, I knew all that. I could pass any exam in nutrition. But somehow, when you're as bad, as desperate as an anorexic feels, none of the scientific facts apply to you. All you deserve is pain, with no excuses. You can't be lazy. And other people need to see it too. They need to see how much you hurt inside.

I did not see Bethany or anybody else besides my nurse. So I perched on the edge of a hard couch and held my muscles in. It was the last obsession and the last safeguard that I could cling to, because nobody could stop me doing it. But it hurt, and I wanted to stop. So I decided that the only person who would shut the Monkey up on this one was the person who had given it the notion in the first place.

So I called my piano teacher. I wrote out a detailed question before I even picked up the phone, because I wanted to get this sorted once and for all: I asked if the things these nurses had said were true. If I really couldn't tone my stomach muscles 'in any position, whether sitting, standing, walking or lying down'. I read back over it. Had I missed anything? Any loophole the Monkey could squirm through? I didn't think so. I used the hospital payphone out in the corridor and read the question. Naturally she agreed with the nurses. Then I found a loophole after all and had to phone her back. She was very kind and patient with me. I have a feeling she knew a thing or two about obsessions and compulsions herself, and I know she felt undeservedly guilty.

Ugly, isn't it? But this is the reality of anorexia. It isn't glamorous; it isn't fun, and often it's accompanied by Obsessive Compulsive Disorder, self-mutilation, bulimia or a whole variety of other demons. The sickness is inside. It's pain and fear and rage. Fear eats you away from the inside out.

Ten per cent of anorexics die. There is no getting around that, no returning from it, no use in its denial. Mental illness can be fatal, and the degeneration of a once bright, happy person is no easier to watch than death by cancer. So don't invite it. Because there is a time (for me, about October) when you know you are playing with fire, when you know it isn't normal any more, but you encourage it for kicks and in hope of thinness. It's the hate-love of the matador for the bull. But it isn't a bull, it's a monkey, and monkeys swing and jump and run and trick you from behind. Then one day they have you by the throat with long, strong, clawing fingers, and you cannot get free any more.

chapter five

Bethany was still the only other patient at the unit.

'They're all on extended leave,' a nurse informed me, 'because it's Christmas.'

Well whoop-de-do, I thought. What did Christmas mean in here? Mainly boredom, emptiness and the absence of a routine. There had been some vague mention of therapy sessions beginning soon, but so far I was still waiting. And it wasn't *Christmas,* anyway, it was Thursday 28 December. That got to me; but not as much as when people said 'it's Christmas' in November: It *isn't.* There's more to life than tinsel and turkey, honestly. Christmas lost its magic when I was nine. It was just after my dad died, but the change was coming anyway. I looked around the world outside our house, and where I had seen magic, joy and sparkle I saw cheesy paper streamers and crumbly glitter ornaments. Where I had seen happy family gatherings before, I now saw frayed nerves as relatives who really didn't *like* each other got together annually, out of duty, with strained lipstick smiles and gaudy Santa hats, children screaming for the flashest toys. People being happy? No, just people getting pissed. The world was too grey to feel happy in. The Samaritans, apparently, get more calls at Christmas than at any other time. In some ways it was even comforting: there was no happy Christmas bubble I had failed to penetrate; I was not the face at the snow-frosted window, because the bubble and the window are *illusions*, unless you're under seven.

While the holiday blank-time went on, Bethany spent many hours in her room, listening to loud music. Nothing abnormal there. When she emerged we would talk – I learned that she was seventeen, liked painting and cats, was an only child and has been self-mutilating for four and a half years.

'I got admitted after I cut too deep one time. I was in school, in the loo, and the blood all came under the cubicle. Some poor Year Seven girl found me.' She grinned guiltily. 'How did they get you?'

'I . . . sort of wanted to come in. Cos I was freaking out.'

'Really?' Her eyes widened. 'You'll regret it. Once the other staff come back and the treatment gets going again, you're in for a rough ride.'

I wandered aimlessly about the unit, always trailed by a nurse. There was just one small corridor in the living quarters. The dining room and then the TV room were on the right-hand side going in, the girls' dormitories at the top end; the place called the community room was on the left. There was a beat-up pool table in there, and a whiteboard, and a hi-fi system that I couldn't get to work. Next to the community room were the toilets; I had discovered that the unit smell came from there. It was the soap: this really pungent, over-powering liquid soap they filled all the dispensers with. I sort of liked the toilets there despite the smell, because they could have been the toilets in any place, in a normal place – no reason to suppose they were the toilets of a secure unit for nutters. I could go in there and, for a moment, just pretend I was an adult working woman out in the world, taking a toilet break from a committee meeting. A woman with an utterly flat abdomen, of course.

There were also a few private bedrooms dotted about. Bethany had one of these. I wondered how it was decided who was given a private room. Those who needed one, or those who'd been here longest? Down the far end of the corridor was the staff room, and then the boys' dormitories. If you turned left there, you went into another corridor. I didn't know where that led, and I couldn't guess. For a while I sat in the TV room. Nothing happening there. So I stared out of the window for a bit. The sky was white and frozen-looking. I kept to the middle of the rooms, as far as possible from the radiators. You burn more calories when you're cold.

Food came over to the unit from the main part of the hospital on a little chugging buggy. It looked just like a golf cart. They sent us steaming aluminium trays, which the unit staff unloaded in the kitchen, behind the hatch and door. You could watch them at it. There was nothing better to do.

At lunch time I tried something I had never eaten in my entire life: boiled cabbage. It was a green vegetable so it must be relatively safe I decided. Eleanor the Troll Woman was supervising and she made me eat a lot of it. It didn't taste too bad. At that meal the Monkey won a minor victory. I had this clementine I was supposed to eat, and I left about half of it concealed in the peel. I held up the peel to show the Troll. She nodded satisfaction; let me put it in the bin. The calories that I had saved were minuscule, even I knew that, but it was a victory of principle: slowly, I was clawing back my power. It sustained me through the afternoon, and as the Troll patrolled, I could smirk silently behind her back, clinging to my secret. She thought she had me sussed, but I knew better. Until tea time, that was.

I chose vegetarian chilli. It was the only way I could escape chips. Naturally I tried the mashing and the spreading and the scattering, but Eleanor was wise:

'All of it.' She glared, leaning towards me, one of her eyes twisting and her nose just inches from my face. 'You're not to leave the table till it's finished.'

I didn't move.

'All of it,' said Eleanor again.

Painfully slowly, I picked up my spoon and continued eating. At that point I remembered that chilli was fattening. Then I got really scared. But she wouldn't let me move until I'd finished it. Bethany was long gone. We were alone. Our wills locked. And beneath the glare of that troll-face, tiny spoon by spoon, it all went down, leaving me with a sick and rock-like feeling in my stomach. Guilt clogged my throat. The Monkey voice of anorexia was raging and screaming at both of us. She, this troll, had taken my control. I clenched my fists at my sides. Control might be compromised, but clinging to the scratchings of my dignity, I left the room in silence.

Mum picked me up in the evening. The Troll was all sick smarminess around her.

'Don't you hate her?' I demanded in the car.

'No,' said Mum, 'I don't.'

I asked her if chilli was fattening. She said the meat kind was – from the fat in the meat. I had eaten vegetarian. I didn't believe her; I had tasted the fat going down, great hefty globules of it.

chapter six

On Friday I met Chloe.

The day began in much the same way: cold and boring. On the way to the unit we stopped at a newsagent's. Mum bought me a pile of magazines with crosswords in, and I had my CDs with me. The CDs were not much good, because I still couldn't get the hi-fi to work. It felt strange to be bought so much at once. I have never been a spoiled child. I'd never asked for things in shops, not even when I was a little girl. Now my mum couldn't buy me enough things, even little things – anything that might make me feel brighter. I was grateful to her, but I felt bad. Guilty. Because this time she couldn't make it better, not with magazines and certainly not with sweets, and she wanted to so badly. It must be a bad thing for parents to feel. I was thirteen. Most anorexics are at least fifteen or sixteen. Young, for the inside of my head to be such a battle-ground. The one place where no one can help you.

I saw Chloe from a distance first. I was in the middle of the corridor, near the doors to the reception. The entire unit formed a sort of cross-shape, with the reception foyer in the middle. The new girl was hefting a large rucksack into the dormitories and did not see me. She was a tall, well-built girl with shiny hair and clear skin: no anorexic then. Later she came into the TV room and flopped down in much the same way Bethany had; but she chose the beanbag.

'Hello,' she said. I was surprised by her voice: a soft, sweet little-girl's voice that belied her robust appearance.

'Hello.' We did the introductions.

'Where do you live?'

She answered: 'Here.'

That killed me.

We clicked right away, Chloe and I, but it was she who sealed the friendship. A little after two o'clock she found me in the community room, still struggling with the hi-fi; she had a look at it, then paused, vanished and returned with her own CD player. 'Use this one. Just leave it here when you're finished with it. I'll collect it later.'

It was a simple gesture that asked nothing in return. I was overwhelmed with gratitude and thanked her many times, but still felt hopelessly inadequate and guilty. Why were all the patients here so nice except for me? Chloe vanished again.

I sat and listened to my CDs, trying hard to keep a straight back and good posture regardless of my piano teacher's words. As far as the Monkey was concerned, whatever would make me slimmer must be good advice; whatever would make me fat and lazy must be bad. I stayed as far as possible from radiators. Then I had a thought. I had seen Chloe looking at a magazine – the unit had some old out-of-date ones – so I left the one I'd had that morning on her CD player for her, with a thank-you note. It was a small gesture back, and inadequate, but I felt the happier for it.

I had dropped off 'levels', but somebody was supposed to check me every fifteen minutes. They didn't. Bethany and Chloe had evaporated, so in the middle of the afternoon I found myself entirely alone. I wandered back to the TV room, although I was already sick of those four walls, and dragged a chair into the very centre – the furthest point from the heating pipes. I faced the window. Outside, it was snowing silently. If it hadn't been for the occasional soft footstep from the far end of the corridor, I could have been all alone in the world.

Aloneness didn't matter – I didn't want to be with anybody. What mattered was the heavy pain inside my stomach, weighted down with food, and the growing sense of captivity. Forgetting my desire to be admitted in the first place, I was suddenly angry, hated everyone for making me come here. *I want to be out in the world,* I told myself. *If I could just be outside I'd be normal.* I pictured myself walking round town, looking at things. No problem. I could do that. *I shall tell Mum not to bring me tomorrow,* I fantasized. *I'll just tell her I don't need this. I shall refuse to come – what right does anyone have to control my life like this?! Fuck them, FUCK THEM, I hate them ALL!*

But anger takes energy, and I was so terribly tired. A heavy, killing tiredness. Outside, the snow was deep and fresh – I watched it drift and shimmer on the window. *I will go to sleep. Go to sleep and make the time go away . . .* But of course it would not last long. In less than an hour it would be tea time, and I would be woken, forced into another battle of wills and wits. I prayed Eleanor had gone off duty.

I sat straight in the chair like a bundle of coiled springs. I could not sleep for a moment.

chapter seven

On Saturday my control over being cold snapped, and I spent fifteen minutes clinging to the radiator. The Monkey in me was irate. I felt depressed, confused, afraid, a failure. I must be getting so fat. Afterwards the skin on my arms was bright red:

'There's strange marks on your arms,' a bland nurse said idly.

'Oh yeah, I wonder how they got there.' I looked down, surprised. 'Maybe because I was beside the radiator.'

'Mm.'

Later, to my horror, I learned they had suspected me of self-harm. It had been entered in my records. In all honesty, it had not yet crossed my mind.

A youngish nurse who evidently knew absolutely nothing about me supervised the lunch. Chloe, Bethany and I ate together. This was a unit rule: everybody had to come to the table at meal times, even if they didn't want to eat. If your problem was not food-related, you could eat or not eat as and when you wanted. I ate a few baked beans, and a bite of baked potato.

'I've had enough,' I tried for the first time, cautiously.

'All right then, mate, no problem!' the nurse exclaimed. He looked surprised at my tentative, humble tone.

My eyebrows shot up. The Monkey whooped for joy: '*All right, kid! Hold the power!*' I strode up to the door and on through to the kitchen, scraped my plate and dumped it in the sink with a decisive clatter.

My mother was allowed to call in later. I had come to long for her visits. Now that she wasn't the one forcing me to eat, she became a shining figures of goodness in my eyes, someone who might ally with me against the tyrants of the unit. Someone who had pity. Adam came once, and sat in the foyer with his head down, blushing and staring at his hands. Occasionally he shot little glances at me, then looked down again. There was no resentment in his eyes, despite my definite monopoly on attention; all I could read in him was sad incomprehension: *What has she become?* I felt sorry for him for having to be there, sorry for exposing him to my shit. He might be older, but he was far too innocent for this.

That afternoon, Mum took me out in the car to the

nearby village. Of course she asked me what I'd had for lunch, and somehow I couldn't lie – which was extremely strange, seeing as I had been lying about food to spare her feelings for the past three months. But suddenly, in this new setting, I apparently couldn't any more. And obviously she was upset:

'I think you know that's not enough,' she said, and in the tone that means: *I'm not angry with you, just disappointed* – which of course is so much worse. It's easier when parents shout, and then it's over with. Drawing that look and that tone out of the people you love is so much harder. So although I'd pacified the Monkey, I now felt guilty on another count. Caught between the hammer and the anvil.

Mum dropped me back at the unit, saying goodbye in the reception lobby. As I was a day patient, she would collect me again at about six or seven o'clock. Looking back, I realize she spent a hell of a lot of time driving back and forth from our house to the unit: once in the morning to take me in, once at night, sometimes in the middle of the day to see me. And thinking about me the rest of the time, as she told me. On top of which she made her daily visits to my nan, now in a home, and suffering from Parkinson's and dementia. Love is a verb.

I hated it so much when she left. When I was very

small I used to go to playgroup in our old church hall. Everybody's mothers stayed for the first half of the session, for the singing and the games and building bricks and tricycles that rattled on the wooden floor. I've seen a photo of myself there, my hair still short, curls barely long enough to pull up on top of my head like a sprig of mistletoe. I am on my hands and knees, clutching a teddy and grinning. I can't have been more than two. But I remember it; most of all I remember the biscuit time. All the toddlers and the little children sat around a table. The mothers sat at the front of the hall, near the stage. They gave you custard creams or malted milk, and milk to drink; for a moment I would be distracted and forget the wrench that was coming. Then I would look up, all of a sudden, at the empty space where my mother should be. It was called adjustment: the mothers were supposed to pop out for a brief time so that we would adjust to separation.

I was a bad adjuster. I cried. Every parting was as hard and scary as the last. There was a nice girl called Victoria a year or two older than me, with hair so pale it was almost white, and pure white skin to match.

'Don't cry!' She always tried to comfort me and share her biscuits. It took a long time for me to accept the parting.

But once I did, I forgot all the fear and pain of it quite suddenly. On my first day of nursery I was as cool as a cucumber. I barely noticed that my mum had left; just made a beeline for the puzzles and sat down to apply my brain. There were other kids who used to cry, who'd never done 'adjustment', but not me. I was fine. Teachers wrote on my reports how mature I was.

Eleven years later, being left at the unit even for a few hours, that same sense of abandonment returned. A psychiatric unit is a *bad* place: the smell is bad, the walls are bad, the food is bad, the air is bad; the sense of bad is primitive, almost animal. You could feel your hackles rise. Threat oozed from the walls and the carpets; I felt it – but whether with the Monkey, or with my real self, or with both, I couldn't tell.

I went back into the corridor of the living quarters. In place of the usual cobwebby quiet, music was pulsing out from the community room. I didn't know the song, but afterwards I found out it was Westlife: 'When You're Looking Like That'. I didn't usually like Westlife – too poppy/boy band/manufactured. But I thought that song was all right. It brought a bit of life to the place anyhow. Broke the deadening air. I headed in the direction of the sound. With the addition of music, the name 'community room' was a little more convincing. A place where some sort of slight community might actually meet.

That's partly why what I found there came as such a shock.

Bethany was lying on the couch, listening to the music, her face streaked with tears. Her arms were exposed, strapped up and padded with fresh white bandages. Crimson stained the sterile white already. She had been cutting herself.

I froze in horror. For a moment I could not believe it – *Why? Why?* My mind fumbled for some other explanation; which was futile – Bethany was *here* because she cut herself. The irony of my reaction was lost on me; I could not comprehend why she would hurt herself, yet I had been punishing myself for months. I was still new there, and naïve. Later I would learn that you came to take such scenes and worse for granted in a psychiatric unit.

I still don't like Westlife. But to this day, I cannot hear that one song without tears welling in my eyes, without seeing Bethany like that again. Bethany, who did not deserve it. I was learning hard realities about the world, and fast.

I stood before her, stunned and stupid. 'Do you want me to leave?' I asked.

She shook her head, so I sat down and listened to the record.

'Nice song,' I said when it was finished. She nodded and gave me a tearful smile. I stayed for a little while, in case she wanted to talk or something. But she was quiet, and I couldn't think of anything to say that wouldn't sound totally futile, so eventually I got embarrassed, mumbled something and went out. Maybe I should've stayed longer. Maybe she wanted me there. Or maybe she was glad I went; she'd been alone to begin with. Or perhaps it didn't matter either way; for here were problems that were maybe even deeper and more deadly than my own, and that was an eye-opener. So I was not the only kid in the world with problems. I wondered what had happened in Bethany's life to make her do that, and why she was blaming herself.

chapter eight

New Year's Eve at the unit.

I begged Mum not to leave me in the morning. But she did – because she had to – she had signed a piece of paper committing me to the unit's care, and they said I must be there. I had not been present at the signing. My mum filled me in a long time later. Jane Wright, that steely bitch, had held it out to her and challenged: 'This is the time that parents always back down.'

My mother said it was one of the most difficult things she'd ever done.

So, New Year's Eve. I shut myself up in the fake library and wrote a bad poem called 'The New Year'. It was a dire drone, and I wept buckets afterwards. Everything felt so pointless, so dull and endless, and I couldn't see how things would ever change for me, no matter how many New Year's Eves there were. Afterwards, Bethany and Chloe and I sat at the table and discussed the New Year or, more specifically, what a bitch it was.

'One more year.' Bethany shrugged. 'Nothing changes.'

'I've decided,' said Chloe very suddenly, 'that the New Year doesn't start until I'm better.' She had not spoken much until that point, but when she did, it was with a startling quiet conviction that I think took us both by surprise.

'That's nice,' said Bethany wistfully. I agreed. We sat in silence for a moment. Chloe gazed at the sky outside. Bethany lowered her eyes. I stared into the middle distance. One by one, we left.

I went home, and slept through midnight.

On 1 January the unit closed, so I was at home all day. Mum said she would take me into town to HMV to spend my Christmas vouchers if I ate a small bowl of cornflakes and a banana for breakfast. I wheedled her down to about three quarters of the cereal, took a couple of bites of the banana and hid a large chunk in a napkin. The last time I had been honest it had only hurt both of us, so I reverted to my old ally, deception. *'Good girl,'* crooned the Monkey. *'Grip that power, kid.'*

In the main street of the town we passed a clothes shop. In the window was a pair of corduroy trousers. I don't have a great deal of enthusiasm for clothes. I pretty much live in jeans, and can rarely be bothered to fiddle with make-up and jewellery. I always thought it unfair that, as a girl, I am somehow expected to take an interest in these things. My mum likes clothes, and sometimes she would drag me through the shops in town, pointing out the things she liked and trying to drum up enthusiasm. Sometimes I would fake it – but in truth, I had eyes only for Waterstone's, which I would watch with longing out of the window, marshalling my patience. But occasionally I'll make an effort, and those cords appealed to me:

'They're nice,' I said noncommittally.

'Would you like to try them on?'

I was surprised; still not used to being offered things out of the blue.

'OK.' But inside the shop, the smallest size was size eight, and they were hanging off me. I stared at myself in the mirror. Victory – triumph – pleasure – anger. I put myself through so much, because the Monkey in me told me I was fat; yet look at this! This evidence! Why was she so hard on me? Right now the little imp was doing backflips out of glee.

'There you are,' said Mum with quiet seriousness, and I realized she had known all along: she had wanted me to try them on to show me something. It worked for about thirty seconds. By the time we left the clothes shop, I was feeling big again.

In HMV I bought a DVD by this cheesy boy band I was

into at the time. I guess they weren't as bad as some manu-factured money-spinners, but I still cringe and grin when I remember my crush on them. I started liking them the moment they came out, when I was eleven. I fancied the lead singer. My feelings confused and embarrassed me, so for a long time I kept it a huge, delicious, guilty secret, particularly from my mum. I didn't think I could stand it if she laughed at me or thought my crush was weird. Funnily enough, my brother knew about it, and I was fine with that; I even messed about and overplayed my crush to make him laugh, but it had to be a secret from my mother. It stayed that way for a while, but after a year or so the band started getting pretty famous, and my mum became aware of them, and obviously noticed that I had all their CDs and junk. If she'd been disdainful I'd have died. I really thought I would have. But to my amaze-ment, she didn't laugh, or even seem surprised. It was she who pointed out the DVD.

'Um, I don't know,' I mumbled, still wanting to conceal the depth of my teenage feeling. 'It's, uh, pretty expensive.'

'Twelve ninety-nine.' Mum shrugged. 'If it will make you feel better, Jess, I'm sure it's worth it.'

Joy! Now I could buy it without seeming idiotic.

'Yeah, OK.' I feigned lightness. Happiness as I left

the store, clutching the DVD in a bag – but as I was about to get back in the car, the Monkey reared up:

'*You haven't done very much walking. You're such a lazy bitch. What exercise have you been doing these past few weeks?*'

So I made the excuse that I wanted to look for a magazine. We stopped at a large newsagent's; I got out of the car and moved about as much as I was able, 'maximizing every movement', like they say in slimming books. Some small relief – the Monkey stopped its roaring and just snarled.

At home we put the DVD on, and my mother was astonished when she saw a smile creep over my face.

'You're smiling!' she exclaimed, and we both started laughing. 'There you are, I told you to buy it!' We were sitting on the floor together in the front room, with cushions and the fire on. I would've given a lot to freeze time there, at that one moment, the two of us laughing together like in the old days, with my band on the television. I was overwhelmed with gratitude to her, with love – oh God, she'd done so much for me, not just that year but every year, especially since Dad died . . .

But time barged on, and I had to return to the unit the following day, and I was too fat for my Monkey.

chapter nine

Next day I was the only patient at the unit. I was taken to the cold room and stripped off for weighing. I was petrified: I had been eating shed-loads. A new nurse called Viv told me I'd lost 0.3 of a kilo, which is about half a pound.

Yeah, my arse, I thought. *Last time you weighed me right after lunch, so of course I was going to be heavier. Any imbecile knows that. Call yourself a medical institution – you can't even weigh a person at the same time twice running. And your height-measuring thing is still broken.* I nodded and got off the scale.

In the afternoon I sat at the dining-room table and played Scrabble with Viv, who was a cheerful redhead. I was fascinated by her jeans, which were at least two sizes too small for her: she must have literally *poured* herself into them. The zipper was a formidable feat of strength. Unfortunately, this gave the impression of her bottom half being disproportionately smaller than her top: a little person's legs attached to a medium person's torso. I had to keep stifling giggles when she stood up. It was raining outside, and halfway through our game the water started dripping through the ceiling. I looked up and saw that the plastering was old and stained and cracked. A damp patch was spreading dark and fast across it. We quickly abandoned the dining room and they called out the plumber. *Crappy NHS*, I thought.

Nobody turned up about the water for several hours, and we could hear it as the afternoon wore on, *drip, drip, dripping* faster in the dining room. My nerves began to grate. Now thunder rumbled outside and rain rattled. *Drip-drip-drip. Drip-drip-drip.* The soundtrack to the loony bin, for our listening pleasure.

No other patients returned for a few days. Some food was forced down me with various threats: 'You'll be admitted as a night patient . . . You won't have any visits . . . We can even feed you through a tube.' But the pressure was no more consistent than the staff, who changed throughout the day, and also through the week. Only fitting in with their duty rota, I suppose, but it was unsettling how every time I thought I was getting to know somebody they vanished. Moreover, I could not fathom any system to it; the changeover seemed to be random. What I really hated was 'agency' nurses, drafted in from the general hospitals to cover short-staffing. Complete strangers, in complete charge of you for an afternoon or so, and then they vanished. Some made me eat and some didn't. Some had one rule over sitting at the table, some had another.

Technically, I had two nurses assigned to me: Clive and Pip. Pip was an elderly, grandmotherly lady. I liked her. She was warm and generous, with big permed hair dyed brown, and smiling-wrinkles. I suppose I missed having a grandmother, though I didn't think that to myself.

Eleanor the Troll was hardest and strictest of all the staff. On one hand, she made me eat the most; on the other, she was as compassionate as granite and as pleasant as a needle through the eyeball. She loved to see me cry and shake over a plate of food, saying with relish, 'I know it's hard – but we have *rules* here, Jessica.'

Around my mother she was always sickly-sweet. 'I know what it's like,' she once lied smarmily to her. 'I have a daughter myself. She's a champion ice-skater already, and she's only nine. They told me to be careful because these girls often get eating problems. But thankfully my children are just fine.' Oh so condescending, and so very very kind. If I was in my mum's position, I might well have punched her for that. We all heard plenty more about her daughter. Her son. Her husband. This award.

That honour. This event. The Troll Woman never shut up for a second about her wonderful perfect family. In front of us – teenagers whose problems were wrenching their families apart like cracking bones. Her wonderful daughter won this competition. Her son's great marks at school. A romantic dinner with her husband. Blah. Blah. Gag. *Just wait till something bad happens to one of you.* I nursed the thought in my brain. *Just wait till something comes along to interrupt your perfect life. We'll see how sorted and wonderful you all are then.* I had never met her husband, and had no particular wish for his demise, but I will wager one thing: if Eleanor had suddenly become a single parent, *she* would not have come and watched her children's plays and concerts, smart without trying, smiling and serene, while the other parents came in two by two. I'd stake a lot on that.

The Troll weighed me again on 4 January. The scales registered a gain of 0.2 pounds. The scales actually weighed in kilos but I automatically translated.

'I've put weight on!' I shrieked.

'You've put on point two, Jessica,' she replied with martyred patience. 'You've put on ounces. What you've done is maintained your weight on what you've been eating, and to be honest I don't know how you've done it.'

115

Shows how much you fucking know! It really was a stupid thing to say. She'd just revealed total ignorance of basic dietary facts: when food is restricted, the body's metabolic rate slows right down to conserve its fat store, putting a stop to the least vital functions like heating and circulation to the extremities. Which is why an anorexic is always cold, and also why crash dieting doesn't work long term. The body *adjusts*. It just sails at half-mast, and the most vital tasks, like keeping the heart and lungs working, will be maintained until the very last. The functions actually shut down in order of necessity. I find that pretty amazing. Anyway, my body had been trained to survive on 300–400 calories a day with excessive exercise and only lost weight slowly, so it was no wonder I maintained my weight at closer to 800. The Troll had just proved she knew nothing about what I needed: how could I trust her not to make me fat? I would never trust her anyway, the bitch. Looking at those bright red numbers, fear came clawing up my mind in waves. Panic. It was out of control. They were taking away my thinness, my safeguard and my hard-won dues. How *dare* they? What *right* did they have?

'*There's only one thing you can put your trust in,*' said the Monkey with a weight of evidence behind her. '*Me. I am consistent. Only I will give you certainty. Now listen.*'

chapter ten

What did I want? Everything. To be in control of my life, to get thin and be good at the same time. To be home and be normal, and to be free of the Monkey. To retain the highs of starvation. Why could I not have all these things at the same time? It wasn't fair.

They had been talking about implementing a meal plan, with sanctions for not complying. The nurses needed pressure to make me finish my meals. So the Monkey thought it best that we kill two birds with one stone: one, to lose the mass of extra fat I'd gained, and two, to obliterate any idea of the meal plan, showing I still had control. So I stopped eating. Totally. Not even a HighLights or Slim-a-Soup like during those days in bed. I'd never done that before, but under the iron rod of the Monkey, the resolution came easy.

After the weigh-in, I rushed to the non-library, my space of solitary refuge. After a while Pip came in to call me for breakfast. I had to be at the unit early enough for them to feed me my first meal.

'No thank you,' I said politely, and explained my resolution to lose weight. Pip didn't look surprised at all; she didn't even argue. She asked me to come to the table anyway.

'They'll put pressure on me to eat,' I said darkly.

'No they won't.'

'If they do I'm leaving,' I warned her.

'They won't,' she said, and bundled me out of the room.

'Morning, Jess!' Viv carolled as we came to the table. 'Cereal you 'ave, isn't it?' She began to get the Weetabix and bowls out.

'Viv,' said Pip with a telling look, and shook her head. 'Not today . . .' This was going to be easy.

More staff piled into the dining room, then later Bethany and Chloe. I sipped on a glass of water and observed. People chattered, laughed, passed the cereal, toast and juices back and forth. Then the hospital sent the hot dishes over, and they were spooned out canteen-style from the hatch: porridge and eggs, bacon, tomato, mushrooms. It all looked greasy and awful. The thought of putting any in my mouth was horrid, distasteful. Everyone ignored me.

When it was over I cleared the table (the better to burn off some fat) and went into the TV room. I found a book to read. My stomach was empty, but I felt calm and in control. Very sane, in fact, and safer. I would be OK. I could control this. I could keep a handle on my body with its disgusting weak want of food, and then I would be strong enough to cope. I was hungry. Then later I stopped being hungry and just felt tired. A strange dull weakness was in all my limbs. I wanted to be hard and strong.

In the afternoon there was a little buzz of preparation: Bethany and Chloe were being taken out to a nearby park, to see the pond all frozen and pretty, to feed the ducks. I woke right up and felt alert.

'I want to come as well,' I said to Pip.

'Of course!' she beamed at me.

'Er, Jessica.' Eleanor the Troll was in the doorway.

Damn.

She beckoned me outside. 'You can't go,' she said to me, which was only what I expected. 'You're not playing by our rules, so we won't give you any privileges.'

'Fair enough,' I answered pleasantly, so happy to be in control. So I wouldn't see any ducks today. Well, big boo-hoo-hoo. I've seen ducks before. My calm acquiescence took her by surprise:

'Well . . . it *is* fair enough,' she said, disconcerted.

'Yes.' I smiled placidly. 'Bye for now.'

It was war. All day long I was high, I was winning. But when my mother came to pick me up, of course they told her; and the sight of her face when I went out to meet her, so sad, so desperate, was like a knife-blade in my heart. So sudden. It stopped me short. For a second I regretted everything I'd done; I could've run back, stuffed my face with biscuits just to take that look off her face. Then the second passed, and the Monkey ruled again, but all the elation was gone from my victory.

On the way home I tried to offer some babbled explanation: it wasn't me, it wasn't my fault, the Monkey made me do it.

'But, Jessica,' said my mum with such deep sadness, 'the Monkey is *part* of you.'

Then we were silent. Because we both knew, then, that however much support I had from outside, ultimately only I could beat, or be beaten by, the Monkey. You can force-feed anorexics; you can restrain depressives from harming themselves. You can drug schizophrenics so they won't be violent. But by fighting the illness in that way, you subdue both the Monkey and the real person together, beating them down, and you cannot break one utterly without breaking the other.

chapter eleven

That was a Thursday. Friday morning I was straight back in the unit. Although I didn't know it, the staff were holding a hasty meeting with consultants and my mother. I ate nothing in the morning, and felt I was becoming a ghost. It wasn't a bad feeling. The silent deadpan air, empty rooms and blank walls suited the feeling. Clocks ticked loudly. The longer I went without food, the purer I became. My stomach was concave; I could hold my fingers in the gap – or run them down my ribs and think of playing a xylophone.

In the blank time, I had begun to think about my father. The frantic ritual of obsession had forced thoughts of the past from my mind, but now they floated freely, the sound of his voice and the warm, spicy scent of his aftershave: I conjured that up to combat the unit smell, although it brought stabs of pain to my chest. *Why aren't you here?* I demanded. *If you had stayed, I would be like I used to be, I would still be like you – everybody used to say I had your kindness, had your love of life, but that wasn't me, was it – it was just you. Now you're gone, they're gone. I'm just a fucked-up girl, sitting here in the loony bin.* I ought to have been crying at these things, weeping with grief; instead there was just a great empty ball lodged somewhere in my chest – it hurt, and it was hollow, and this was all I could feel.

At lunch time I ate a spoon or two of cooked carrot. Afterwards I phoned my mum.

'Did you have lunch?' she asked.

'Yes.'

'What did you have?'

'Carrot.'

'And?'

'That's it.' My stomach sank.

'Goodbye.' She hung up. So then I knew that I was totally alone, without even my mother any more.

Saturday and Sunday I ate minuscule amounts. Everybody had turned cold to me by that time, even Pip. If I'd just started eating, it would all have changed. But no one at the unit spelled that out to me – I still hadn't had any therapy – and though I had an inkling, I was so confused, so desperate that I couldn't work it out. An inkling is not strong enough to hold against a Monkey.

So on Sunday night I sat on the end of my makeshift bed in the granny flat and started to cut myself. Now here was a fast change. The week before, I had been so horrified by the idea, I could not work out why people did it to themselves. But now I needed to do something, to try something to ease the pain, and I suppose I thought there must be something good in cutting, if others did it. To hell with tomorrow. I could be dead by tomorrow anyway, so who cared?

I only used some nail scissors. You can't do too much damage with them. First I was just scratching on the surface of my left hand. The little prick of pain felt good, felt like relief. All the pain and shit inside me was suddenly physically manifest. Physical pain I can do. It's easier to manage than the inner wrenching turmoil. I know that's the cliché of self-harm, but if you think like that, it really seems to work. So then I opened the scissors and started stabbing the back of my hand. Then the blood came in a small stream. That felt even better. The look of blood was clear and understandable. Then I stopped. What had I done? Guilt like ice in my belly. This surely, surely wasn't right! It was no game!

Hastily I hid the scissors, planned to keep it secret. But I made no real effort to disguise the cuts, and my mother soon saw them.

'What did you do?'

I froze in the doorway. Scared, remorseful, I stuttered that I'd banged my hand on the door.

'When?'

'Yesterday.' *What?*

'So why is it bleeding now?'

'Um, I, I, hit my hand – and it opened up again.'

'So now you're lying as well.'

'OK,' I blurted angrily. 'I did it myself.' Why did she want truth out of me when lies were easier? *Just leave me. Let me lie myself to death.*

Adam is two years older than me. We've had a decent relationship. Of course, we've squabbled growing up, but mostly we've been good friends and shared a lot of fun times. As kids, we made up games. One favourite was Hang the Barbie. This involved creating complex mechanisms of ping-pong balls, levers and pulleys, the culmination of which was the execution of a Barbie doll. The more elaborate, the better. Other games included Haunted Room, Puppy-in-my-Pocket Death-match and Card Bomb. These activities must have vented all our violent urges, because our school reports always recorded how completely non-aggressive we both were. And we didn't fight.

When Adam and I were small we loved the park. Our mum could occupy us for entire afternoons, just letting us roam in the bushes, exploring the jungles of distant planets, discovering tropical islands. We had a boat, a plane, a rocket ship – Adam was always the captain, but that was fair enough – he was the older brother and as long as I could be his sidekick, I was happy.

Sometimes we sat under a tree and ate sweets. When I was about five, and he seven, we had a craze for the sweets called Warhammer. No relation to the game, as far as I know. Warhammer sweets came in two varieties: hot strawberry and bitter lemon. One tasted like a burning bonfire and the other like stinging vinegar. They were supposed to taste like that: it was an endurance test. You had to suck them for as long as you were able. On the back of the packet was a sort of scoring table:

5 SECONDS	POOR, DUDE, POOR
10 SECONDS	STAY WITH IT
15 SECONDS	WE KNOW YOU'RE SUFFERING
20 SECONDS	ALMOST THERE . . .
25 SECONDS PLUS	*CONGRATULATIONS! YOU ARE A WARHAMMER WARRIOR!*

Well, who wouldn't want to be a Warhammer Warrior? I could never get past ten. I did better with hot strawberry; the lemon killed me. We adored them. Adam held out longer than I did: he was almost a Warhammer Warrior.

'Argh – it hurts!' he would blurt out finally, spitting the sweet into the grass at around twenty – then we would shriek with laughter and watch as the ants gathered, black invaders on a shiny yellow surface. 'Your go.' Adam handed me the packet.

I would brace myself, swill my saliva around – we told each other this was for protection – and take the next sweet onto my tongue, savouring the burn. Because here's the strange thing: those sweets really *hurt*. They actually hurt your tongue, and the inside of your mouth. We loved it. When they put 'suffering' on the packet they weren't joking.

Pleasure/pain is a fine line, and you don't have to be crazy to admit that. Children are more honest about that sort of thing, as they are in most matters. I know loads of people who used to stick pins and stuff in their fingers for fun. When my mum was small, she and her siblings used to give themselves stitches: threading a needle and passing it through the top layers of skin on their hands. My brother and I used to trap our fingers in metal hairgrips as a different endurance test, and shriek with laughter and pain. Adam's friend had a quiz-show buzzer which sent an electrical jolt up your arm. But that's a different kind of fun, and it's mostly experimentation.

Looking back, I think that's really what I was doing on the bed that day, with only a slightly more sinister slant. I *am* better at dealing with physical pain than mental. I've never liked to make a fuss. Aged eleven, I took the skin off half my leg by rollerblading down a huge hill and meeting a stick halfway. I shouted one obscenity then took myself in hand.

Real self-harm – the razor-blade and kitchen-knife sort – is about releasing an inner welt of pain, and it's about punishment, and it's also a cry for help. It's saying to people: *Look how much pain I am in.*

I did not self-harm in a serious way. In fact, I didn't try it again. I wanted to keep pain more secret than that. Got to be steely, not weak.

chapter twelve

On Tuesday 9 January the other kids came back.

There seemed to be so many – twenty, maybe, but in my isolated state it seemed a mass. Boys and girls went up and down the corridor, hefting bags and backpacks, talking to each other and the staff. Tall, short, thin, fat, cheerful and depressed. That at least was interesting. A large boy with a kind and innocent face. A tiny girl with tightly curled yellow hair and strange eyes. The pretty girl who had smiled at me on that visit before Christmas. It seemed an age ago now. An older boy, who greeted Bethany with kisses. Suitcases and rucksacks were swung here, there, everywhere. My eyes opened at the new life and my spirits rose; it might have been the return to summer camp. A grim one.

Suddenly a bell was rung, and the nurses started tramping up and down the corridor and calling, 'Time for school!'

School?

Wait just a minute! The one good thing about the unit was that I escaped school. I still hated school with a passion. But as it turned out, that mystery corridor I hadn't been down yet housed the unit school: I could scarcely believe that nobody had told me about it. The school was just two classrooms and a 'creative room': a largish, art-room place with paints and easels. One classroom was small and one was larger; but, to my delight, the shelves were lined with books. All kinds of books: storybooks, school books, textbooks. I can't describe the relief. Cramped desks and pots of pencils, plants on the windowsill. Even a couple of computers with curriculum programs.

I love to learn. I like to know things, find things out, to understand. I don't like to be disturbed or interrupted while I'm working and I don't like being held back. Obviously that's a part of why I hated comprehensive school so much. Back in Year Eight I had felt so stressed: we had lessons when the teacher didn't turn up and the class went wild. In tutorials (I didn't even know what we were meant to do in those), feeling scared and stressed, I'd get my homework out. Other kids would pull it off me, chanting, 'Homework is for home!' They would throw the pieces of paper to one another. They didn't mean it to be cruel, but I had to fight back tears.

It wasn't the worst kind of bullying. I mean, they never beat me up or stole my money. But I was oversensitive; and with my grandmother declining fast at home at that time, I had no refuge. On top of that, the girls I had been friends with were suddenly plunged into the backstabbing make-friends/break-friends drama of the adolescent female. So between one thing and another it had been a long time since I'd had the chance to really learn anything. Seeing those books and those desks, the pictures and the poems on the wall, I decided I must give the unit school a chance. Maybe it could even be my haven.

I was put in a class with Chloe. The teacher was a sweet but very nervy woman called Janet. There were about five of us in the class; some went to the other teacher, some were on the computers, others went to therapy or different places according to their treatment. My plan of therapy still hadn't been presented to me, and I soon found out there was no plan of schoolwork set out for me either. My own school had not sent any yet. So I sat down at my desk and wrote a story.

It was quite a random story about a girl who's scared to go into a basement. But I can lose myself completely reading or writing, so I was quiet and contented for a while. I liked it in the schoolroom; it was peaceful, and the pressure eased, and the bad smell of the unit was more faint and far away. When I finished writing, I talked to Chloe for a while. I told her they were going to put me on a meal plan, for so the rumour went.

'They haven't given me a target weight,' I said: it was something bothering me.

'No, they won't do that yet.' A new voice came from across the room. I looked up, startled, to see who had spoken. A tiny girl, smaller even than the pretty one, was looking calmly back at me. Her eyes were almost black, though they say that's not possible, and her hair raven-dark. I did not know how to answer her. In truth, I think I was scared. Small she might be, but in her level gaze and the firm set of her jaw was something hard as flint; not malicious or aggressive, but old and torn and very very strong. Her gaze told me: *You have seen nothing, child. You think you have suffered. I know better.* I believed it. Behind those damaged eyes were things I shrank from.

At lunch I watched her eating – slow, painstaking, but determined. She was thin; not skeletal – there was a little weight about her hips and thighs, although her top half was skinnier. She was considerably less than five foot tall; I'd guess four foot nine. Close to, she had features like a pixie, small and delicate. But those eyes held nothing of fairy tales.

Everyone was at the table for the lunch, and it felt livelier and friendlier. These were troubled teenagers, I knew, but people with mental disorders are more than the sum of their problems. They're people, still alive and trying, with personalities and minds and likes and dislikes quite apart from their illness. There *is* hope in youth, I think, and at that particular meal I felt more uplifted than I had in a very long while. I actually ate: a sandwich and a yoghurt. Someone praised me and it felt quite good. I kept watching the dark girl: so small, so hard, so grave. I was curious. I was nervous of her but my fascination got the better of me. When only a few people – all anorexics and their supervisors – were still left at the table, I moved over to sit next to her.

'Hi. I'm Jessica.'

Her very red lips smiled at me but she didn't soften. 'I'm Manda.'

I told her, 'I – I'm anorexic too.'

A smile flickered on her face, more genuine than the first. 'I know – I saw that.'

'Well, they say I am,' I amended. 'But I don't think so. I mean, I just ate a sandwich and a yoghurt for lunch, how am I anorexic?'

She grinned openly at me, and it was startling. 'I know what you mean.'

I faltered. 'So . . . does it get easier or . . . ?'

Manda held up one small hand and tilted all her fingers left to right and back again, an indication that the answer lay somewhere between yes and no. Then, to my complete surprise, she looked me straight in the eyes and asked, 'What's the lowest you've ever weighed?' Just like that. As matter-of-fact as if she'd asked the weather forecast.

'Well, I – I'm at it now!' I answered.

'What's that?'

'Six stone and four pounds.' I paused. That didn't sound too bad. At least it ought to show her that I wasn't such a child after all. 'And what's yours?'

'Four and a half stone,' she said calmly. My mouth dropped open. God, I was an amateur! 'They put a tube up my nose to feed me.'

'That's – that's terrible!' I cried. 'And how tall are you?'

'Five – just under five foot,' she replied untruthfully, and turned back to the remains of her own sandwich. She didn't do my act of scraping and smearing, even though no one was watching her that closely.

I was allowed to carry my plate out to the kitchen. Then I returned to the school.

*　　*　　*

I liked a lot of the kids at the unit. There was a great mix of them. The boy that Bethany went out with was named Robert. He was seventeen. He was clever and quite quiet and sardonically funny. He and Bethany were clearly very happy together. Robert also had scars on his arms, but they were different to Bethany's. Deeper, darker and less clean. He had not scratched himself with blades, but gouged himself repeatedly with some blunt instrument like a wooden clothes peg.

The pretty girl I had noticed the first time I came to the unit was named Sally. She was Manda's best friend, so close they almost seemed to have a secret language. They were always together, their heads bent, dark and tawny hair mingling together, talking quietly. Each seemed to know the other's past. They walked the corridors together, and sometimes it seemed as if Manda were guiding Sally, one hand on her friend's arm or tight around her waist, those strange eyes searching out a path for both of them, treading warily. I won't deny that I was slightly jealous of that friendship: I am not an exclusive, best-friend type, but I thought it might have made it easier, always having a single person to confide in. Unrealistic, really. I make my confessions on paper.

These kids were all different, from so many backgrounds, with varying hobbies and interests . . . but they were nice. Pleasant, generous, intelligent people. So what were they doing in a psychiatric unit?

You can be too nice. One of the major factors in a mental disorder is guilt: and a sense of guilt goes with being too hard on yourself, and not hard enough on other people. I used to be like that when I was young. All my report cards said what a nice girl I was. Pleasant, quiet, passive. I have changed. I am not horrible, like I was when I was actually ill, but I am harder. If somebody lashed out at me, when I was young, I would be angry with myself for deserving such treatment. Now I get angry with people. It is one of my regrets: that I will never be as nice again as I was pre-anorexia. But that kind of blinkered niceness goes with innocence, and it doesn't equip you for life.

chapter thirteen

12 January. My breasts had all but disappeared; I could count every single rib right down my sides and back; my thighs were the same width as my knees. I don't know if I was still trying to lose weight. I think I was just terrified of putting any on. With my anorexic choice of food, the pounds still slid off very very slowly. I got to the unit feeling physically terrible, and decided I must have some bug or virus, though I couldn't work out what. It simply would not register in my brain that starvation is eventually a killer; that at last, after all my months of self-abuse, my body was beginning to give up on me.

I lay down in one of the private bedrooms that was not yet occupied 'to have a nap'. A proficient student nurse with a nose-piercing was assigned to watch me. It was dark. Mid-morning, I stumbled out of bed to go to the toilet; but halfway down the corridor a thick brown murk slid down across my vision, and the next thing I remember I was on the floor. The wall was next to me.

'Jessica!' The student's voice sounded distant. 'What are you doing?'

'I'm . . . um . . . going to the toilet.' *Was that right?*

'OK, well, look, you've passed it.'

I looked up and, sure enough, the girls' toilet door came into focus, back along the corridor the way I'd come. *Shit*, I thought in wonder. *How did that get over there?*

'Come on back to bed now,' the student coaxed me in a gentle voice, as if I were a puppy.

I think I did get to the toilet – then I went to lie down on the bed again, and dropped into a half-sleep. Later in the day, another nurse came in to tell me that 'the team' had had a meeting, and they wanted to admit me that day – as an inpatient. Pretty much there and then. They wanted to monitor me 24/7 now, withhold access to my family if necessary. Oh God, rage! *How dare they? How in the fuck do they dare?* Red klaxons screamed and flashed. It was all spiralling out of control again, it was all falling apart. When in my life had I held onto anything? How could anything be sure?

'You have no right!' I shrieked, trying to get out of the bed. 'You can't control my life, you can't, I'm *thirteen*!'

When the nurse left I hurried to the payphone.

'Mum! You won't believe it – they want to admit me!'

'I know, Jessica, and we've come to an agreement. You will have the weekend to try and gain some weight; otherwise I'll agree to admit you.'

So the next day, Saturday, I tried. I really tried. I had some cereal, and something cooked at lunch. After two meals: '*Oh God!*' cried the Monkey. '*You pig! You're going to be absolutely massive!*' No one was paying much attention to me at tea. Chloe, Manda and another girl were at the table; Eleanor Troll was in charge. Manda wasn't eating anything. No smearing, scraping, messing it about – when she refused to eat she refused outright. I got a slice of bread out of the breadbin, and a piece of ham, and was planning to sit quietly and hope no one noticed me, but with Manda sitting there, her head down, and everybody coaxing her – 'Just a *bite*' – I felt really bad for her and put in:

'Look, I've had a half sandwich, that's all I can manage.' What I meant to convey was: *It won't kill you.* Surely for Manda to eat *something* would be better than nothing at all?

'*Jessica!*' roared the Troll; my heart stalled. 'What you eat has *nothing* to do with what Manda eats! Just because

138

you only had half a sandwich doesn't mean *she* will!' Her features twisted terribly, her eyes bulged. She stabbed a finger at me as she screamed like a manic schoolteacher. I thought she was going to leap over the table and attack me. I *hate* being shouted at; I hate it. I never was at home, and hardly ever at school. Even when I'm angry with someone, I don't shout at them. It just makes things worse.

'Fine,' I replied coldly, inwardly seething with fury. What in the hell had I said that had set her off like that? Manda started crying and ran away; Chloe hyperventilated; Eleanor continued roaring accusations at me. My throat clogged up. Inside, grief and anger choked me; far from being able to eat any more for tea, now I felt like I was going to throw up. Involuntarily, that is.

The Troll barked, 'Everybody is to leave the table. Now!'

I escaped to the empty community room, threw myself down on the couch and sobbed with sorrow and rage. I hated her, loathed her! The *bitch*! She *and* her perfect family could take a long walk off a short cliff and so much the better for everyone. I was racked with fear and guilt: was Eleanor right? Had I done something wrong? Had I now hurt Manda? Somehow made it harder for her to get better? I had only been trying to help her, but the Troll's awful bawling left me ravaged with self-blame. What had I said that was so bad? Then I felt guilty on another count: for not having eaten *enough*, of all things. But now my chest and throat were so tight I couldn't breathe. My mum and I were allies once again – she really didn't want me to sleep there, and I was desperate to please her. So I went and got a strawberry yoghurt, looked at it, then ate it by myself.

When my mum came to collect me, late in the evening, the Troll had gone home to her lair. A compassionate nurse let my mum into the main part of the unit so she walked into the dining room. Inspiration struck. I held up the biscuit I was crumbling to pieces and said, 'From now on, I'm only eating for my mum.' And then I ate it. 'Look, Mum, I did it!' And in the car: 'I'm only eating for you,' I repeated. 'If they keep me in the unit I'll eat nothing.' I was babbling, and I could hear it myself. Coming totally unravelled. But the sole thought in my head was: *Stay out of that place!* My mum was utterly confused. I had just eaten a biscuit in front of her and I pressed my advantage: 'I'm only eating for you, Mum! Keep me at home with you!'

'But you won't eat,' she said.

'Yes! I just did! For you!'

'Yes, but . . .' She shook her head, bewildered, as cars zipped by on the road. I was huddled in the back seat, sitting sideways like a child out past its bedtime.

'But you have to eat for yourself,' she protested.

Eat for myself? How utterly alien. How could I do that for myself, the only thing I didn't want to do? I begged her and begged her not to take me back on Monday morning. It did not work.

First of all, they weighed me. They made me strip to knickers and bra. If anorexics are allowed to be weighed even in light clothes they will often hide a heavy belt beneath the clothing, wear chunky jewellery, even fill their pockets with gravel and small stones. Our shaky dial scales at home were vague from pound to pound, but these were the business. They measured to a 0.1 of a kilo. I was even made to take off my watch.

I saw that I had lost another half-kilo – in my language, one pound. First I was encouraged by the Monkey's praise, then the realization hit me: I was going to be here in the night from now on and I cried for pretty much the whole day.

I wandered up and down the corridor, sobbing; the walls blurred. The Troll watched with malignant satisfaction. She wore a tight leather jacket in the ugliest, most vulgar shade of pink I've ever seen.

'Jessica.' Chloe hurriedly came up to me and held my forearms, forcing me to look into her face. 'You remember – when was it? – last night, when you said you ate that biscuit for your mum?'

'Yeah,' I answered tearfully, and snivelled.

'Well,' she continued, her coffee-coloured eyes wide and brimming with sincerity, 'I'm *here*, getting better, for *my* mum.'

'Y-you are?'

'Because I love her.'

'And I love mine too.' Once again, she had given me something to cling to.

I got a poky side room – one of the private ones – for which I was thankful. The bed was high and hard, with regulation green hospital sheets. 'NHS' and the hospital name were printed on the bottom. Beside the bed was a thin wardrobe. A battered chair was set on the other side. The window looked onto a portion of the car park and some trees behind it. The trees were good to see. The walls of the room had a sickly, greenish-grey tint. The bad smell was strong.

I cried myself to sleep that night, with images of home and Bethany's Westlife song playing on a loop inside my head.

PART THREE:
WRESTLING

chapter one

I slept deeply all night long. In the morning I awoke, surprised. The world had not stalled on its axis overnight. In fact, the sun was shining and the sky was pale blue. Somehow that was heartening. I got up, dressed, washed at the sink in the toilets and waited to see what would chance.

My school had at last sent some work for me, with some very nice notes from my teachers. But that was the furthest thing from my mind. That day, my first as an inpatient, the staff drew up a meal plan for me:

BREAKFAST	2 WEETABIX WITH 200ML SEMI-SKIMMED MILK, 200ML ORANGE JUICE, BANANA
MORNING BREAK	200ML ORANGE JUICE, 1 PORTION FRUIT
LUNCH	COOKED MEAL AND PUDDING FROM HOSPITAL MENU

AFTERNOON BREAK	YOGHURT, 100ML SEMI-SKIMMED MILK
TEA	1½ ROUNDS OF SANDWICHES (I.E. 3 SLICES BREAD), YOGHURT
SUPPER	200ML MILK OR MILKY DRINK, 2 BISCUITS

Less than most teenagers ate, my mother told me, but considering how light I was and how sedentary they kept me in the unit, it was supposed to make me gain a pound a week. Needless to say, I ignored it. Well, not quite ignored. It was decided – in no small part due to my own wrangling – that I would sit at the table with whatever food was on the plan in front of me for half an hour. If I didn't finish – which was always – I would have to sit there for another half-hour, doing nothing, when everybody else was gone. Then I would be released – the unit schedule had to carry on: I had school. I hated that detention period:

'It feels like a punishment,' I snivelled, 'even though I'm trying my hardest.'

'It's not a punishment,' a friendly nurse assured me. 'We don't have punishments here.'

But Eleanor Troll disagreed: 'Well, yes, it is punitive, Jessica, because that's the only card we've got to play.'

Oh, give the woman a round of applause. What a move.

Telling people locked into a self-loathing, self-punitive and selfish cycle of destruction that they are being punished. Bravo, Troll. Everyone hated her. We all bitched about her the moment she went out of the room. Well, perhaps that's not quite fair. As Manda once put it, 'I don't think anyone who does this job could just be purely bad.'

'But she *is* a bitch,' said someone else, and we started laughing. It was that *perfect family* stuff!

'But do you think it's true,' I asked my mother a long time afterwards, 'that nobody who does that job could be all bad?'

'It might be, Jess.' She was not to be drawn.

I was adamant: 'I think that any job – any position of authority – can be abused. It's all a power trip.'

'The other point,' she said astutely, 'is that Eleanor kept repeating all those things about her children and her husband. As though she was trying to convince herself. Maybe it wasn't all so perfect.'

My eyes widened; there was a thought.

At the end of that day I retreated to my little room, sat on the bed and totted up my calories. I guessed that I had eaten:

2 Weetabix	130
120ml semi-skimmed milk	60
10ml orange juice	5
3 oz potato	75
Veggie thing	100?
Yoghurt	50
2 slices bread	122
Ham	45

That came to 587 calories. Surprisingly non-inflated. Then I thought that if I ate all the supper in the evening it would come to 805. I wasn't sure how I felt about that. Relieved? Or disappointed? Was I *disappointed* they weren't making me try harder? But you can't make somebody, of course, without breaking them. Or was I scared; that I would put weight on having eaten just the little that I'd had? Most of all I guess I was surprised. I had thought it would be more than that. I hid my pen and diary beneath the mattress.

Supper was supposed to be at nine, but I wanted mine half an hour early so I could escape to my room. I have never liked late nights, and always need to read before I sleep. The night-nurse Ruth appeared to consent readily enough, but recorded it without my knowledge. Apparently I showed a lack of willingness to conform to unit regulations. (*Well, God in heaven forbid! If this lackadaisical attitude continues, we'll have people pouring out the cornflakes at 8.01 instead of eight o'clock, brushing their teeth at all sorts of unholy hours. Oh Lord, quell the mob lest anarchy seize us all!*)

Ruth and I sat at the dining-room table alone and I crumbled my digestive biscuits, pretended to sip at the milk with my lips tight closed. Ruth talked to me – what I now thought of as *Tales from the Outside World*. I listened. She had a dazed and sombre manner and her eyes were sad. A bit like a depressive. Well, they do say that practically all mental-health workers have been in treatment themselves, so you never know. Presently her eyes went wide and she remarked: 'You've been eating that as I've been talking to you!'

I looked down, and was alarmed and frightened by how low the milk looked, and how much of the biscuits had somehow gone into my mouth.

'That's bad,' I heard myself say.

'No, that's good!' said Ruth.

I clamped my lips tight shut and not another morsel passed them. One day in, and already they were stealing my control.

Things were strange at night. Agency nurses I had not met wandered up and down the corridor like phantoms. Sounds echoed. Sometimes you could hear crying in the night. I was scared.

chapter two

Back before Christmas, I had wanted to escape from my house, where the monster was eating me up. *If I could get out of here*, I had thought, *somehow change the situation, I would be free of it.* I'd been wrong. Now I found that I had brought the monster with me, inside: the Monkey squirmed and wriggled in my brain, beating the walls of my skull.

The days had more structure now. I was roused at eight by a knock at the door and a nurse calling, 'Jess!' No matter if you felt like shit, you still got up at the same time. I'd dress, brush my teeth and struggle through breakfast. There was no hiding up in your room – you had to face the community at the table. One by one, we got called to the clinic for morning medication, which they handed out in tiny plastic cups. I still got the Prozac, and also a cream for my skin. Because I hadn't eaten fats for so long, my knuckles, knees and elbows had dried, cracked and bled like an outbreak of badly scratched eczema. Then school – interrupted for lunch and for personal or group therapy as scheduled.

Group was usually pretty quiet. We sat in a ring with two therapists who tried to get us talking about our difficulties – sometimes we said nothing, other times we would wander off on a tangent and end up giggling. My personal therapist was a petite, nervy woman named Louise – we had our meetings in an office-like room with a whiteboard. The first thing she did after introductions was offer me a cup of herbal tea:

'Er, no thanks.'

'There aren't any calories in it.'

I grinned ruefully. 'It's not that' – I was telling the truth – 'I don't really drink tea.' *Especially not tea with flowers in it. Flowers just aren't for consumption.* 'But thanks anyway.'

'So how are you, Jessica?'

'Fine, thanks.' The finer I was, I supposed, the sooner I'd get out of there.

'Are you settling into the unit?'

I shrugged.

'How are you getting along with the other patients?'

'Fine. Everybody is really nice.'

'Good! I'm so glad. So tell me, Jessica – is there anything you'd like to talk about today?'

'Nope. Not really.'

'Then is it OK if I ask you some questions?'

Another shrug. I played primary school with Louise deliberately: my name is Jessica. I'm thirteen. I live with my mother, my brother and our cat. Our cat's name is Alfred. She inspired no confidence in me – I judged her weak and timid, a victim-type. Imagine trying to tell her of my efforts to detach my body from physical pain, using the force of my mind! Impossible. When she broached the subject of my father I got angry: *Oh no. Don't talk about him. I don't want this place, or you people, invading my good time, my pure time.*

Next: 'I have a little exercise for you.' Louise gave me a pen and asked if I would draw myself, as I saw myself, on the whiteboard.

Well, come on, I'm not dumb, I thought straight away. *They're all harping on about how underweight I am; so if I draw myself as fat they'll think I'm crazy. Sheesh. Give my intelligence a little credit.* So I drew myself as small and slim; and smiling. I can't draw for beans, incidentally, so my sketch looked pretty childish. But I got my point across. Louise looked at my picture with an approving nod. I almost started laughing. Louise and I were getting nowhere, slowly.

After school it was tea time, then visiting hours. Visitors had to be out by eight o'clock – to the second, if the

Troll was on duty. Some people's parents hardly ever came, and I felt bad for them – all those hours of blank time, of sitting and waiting and thinking. Later people congregated in the community room or else retreated to their rooms. I hated the way my time was ruled to the minute, every second of every day, but I hated the blank weekends more. Anorexics only got leave if we put a pound on – otherwise, we stayed. Then the unit was so quiet and so empty, like the holidays; enough grey walls and ticking clocks could drive anybody insane.

When Mum came in to visit me on Tuesday evening, we sat in the fake library together. She said that my friend Rachel had come by the house that day and told me to please get better. I was pressed against the radiator, silent and sullen and blank-faced. Mum was sitting near me.

'Look at this!' she cried, pointing to my thigh. 'Your legs are straight, quite straight from knee to hip. There's no curve there at all!'

I did not see what was bad about that: I had child's legs now, just like I wanted, just like the Monkey wanted. But I was afraid that my mum's visits would stop. I wasn't adhering to my meal plan and Eleanor had threatened that, if this continued, I wouldn't be allowed to see my mum. Her visits were the only thing that was keeping me going. I had a review scheduled for the next day and was terrified the Troll would seize the chance to ban them: the prospect of being alone, all alone, without an ally in the cold world of the unit was enough to breed thoughts of suicide.

'I can count all your ribs,' Mum went on, 'just by looking at you.' Then she cried.

Her tears hammered my defences. They combined with a miserable day at the unit, news of Rachel and the brief play of sunlight on trees I'd glimpsed from my bedroom window. These changed something inside me very suddenly.

Realization hit me. I was under seven stone. *Way* under, in fact. And at seven stone, I had been as happy with my body as I could ever be. I hadn't always looked repulsively fat to my reflection – and that was probably the best I could hope for, under the Monkey. So I might as well be seven stone again. I had never, ever allowed myself to gain weight since the start of that diet in the summer. If I put on one pound in the week, I could go home for two nights at the weekend. That was the unit rule. *Go home.* Now the idea seemed like paradise.

'Mum,' I said suddenly, 'I'll eat all my meal plan till the weekend. I'll get to seven stone.'

'*But you can't be more than seven stone,*' the Monkey wailed. '*Any more than that, you'll be huge!*'

'OK,' she said tearfully, not believing me of course.
'No, really!' I exclaimed.

She looked at me. I don't know what in my face or tone convinced her, but there must have been something there. We hugged and laughed and cried and pretended to kick the anorexic Monkey to death. That was only symbolic. Of course, it wasn't dead.

The slide into anorexia is a process; so is the hard climb out. What I had done was hit the bottom of the pit – I probably was there the day the GP had stood over me and watched me trying to do sit-ups – and lingered there a while. Brooding in the dark and blending with the Monkey. Now, by my first stand against the monster's will, I'd turned my face towards the sunlight at the top of the cliff before me. But the cliff still had to be climbed; and the Monkey would be grappling and scrabbling at me every step of the way, desperate to pull me back down to the bottom again, where it could live and be strong. Already it sprang up at me, issuing threats.

'If – if I stick to the meal plan tomorrow, and tonight, will I be more than seven stone by Thursday's weigh-in?'

'No, you won't,' said Mum.

'Promise?'

'Promise.'

I don't think those who called themselves professional would have approved of this. Personally, I think it is all right to promise sometimes, in the very beginning, if things are as sure as they can be. The revelations will come later. Maybe a long time afterwards.

So I turned to a fresh, blank page in my diary and we wrote on it:

As of now (6.41 p.m., 16 January) I, Jessica, will eat everything on my meal plan until Thursday when I am weighed, even though drinking 400ml of orange juice and 500ml of semi-skimmed milk a day seems disgusting.

I will have my supper tonight and I will have pudding tomorrow, but it is what I need to put on the right amount of weight to be slim and healthy.

Underneath my mother added: Witnessed by Mum.

She stayed most of the evening. The day staff were preparing to go home.

'Ask for supper early,' my mum encouraged me, 'so I can stay a minute and hear you've had it!'

So I went and found the vacant-eyed nurse Ruth, and we sat down at the table together. She heated milk for me and got the two digestive biscuits out. I tucked into them at once. The biscuits went down quite fast. When the milk was about halfway gone and the glass at my lips, the Monkey screamed in agony:

'*You pig! What the fuck are you doing?*'

'*Go to hell,*' replied the other voice exuberantly, quite delighted and convinced it would all be easy from then on.

'You've done very well,' Ruth said in a dazed voice, a look of complete confusion on her face. She meandered out again, utterly perplexed.

I chuckled to myself and put the plastic cup and saucer in the sink. Then I sauntered back into the non-library.

'Did you do it?' asked Mum eagerly.

'Of course I did,' I answered.

She hugged me. Then visiting time was over. We kissed goodbye in the foyer and I strode back to my room, filled with confidence. Everything was going to be OK from now on – I could beat this. Tomorrow we'd show everyone how well I had this monster under control. They'd believe us – they *had* to believe us! Then I'd go home, and pretty soon I'd be well again. I fell asleep smiling.

chapter three

The review was dire. We all trooped back into the office where I'd been on my first visit there. My two nurses Pip and Clive, Jane Wright the cold psychiatrist, Julie the dietician who had issued the meal plan, the consultant Fred, Fireman Sam, my mother and I. One by one, they made their reports on me: all drear, all dark, all damming. I was not adhering to my meal plan. I was not following unit policy. I was, in general, doing very badly and was in fact very bad.

'But – but—!' I stammered. 'I'm eating now!'

Breakfast had gone fine that morning. I'd suppressed the Monkey successfully and eaten the food up. But my stomach had shrunk through starvation; the sheer bulk of Weetabix and milk felt leaden-heavy inside. It was an uneventful meal. We put the dishes away, snored through a humdrum meeting and went down to the classroom. I did some of the work from school, and it made me feel good; more normal. Mid-morning I went and ate my snack with Sally and Manda. It went down without much fuss. Even the pudding at lunch. No gateau or pie and cream – I ate my little custard tray with plastic skin on top. I was eating, I *was* eating—

'Yes, we know,' said Jane Wright harshly. 'That's good. But you haven't been, have you, Jessica?'

My cheeks burned. I looked down at my thin hands and felt tears well in my eyes.

'I will be seven stone,' I told them with pathetic dignity. Nobody answered so I later said it again. They talked on and on about food and adherence.

'Yes, I will continue eating,' I replied. 'Until I'm seven stone.'

'I think Jessica needs to take on board,' said Julie the dietician, 'that nobody's agreed to this weight of seven stone.'

'Well, how much do you want me to be?'

'We'll have to see, Jessica, we're not sure yet, because everybody's different.'

'I will be seven stone,' I said again.

'I think that would be a good interim target,' said Julie.

I ground my teeth. 'What are you thinking of?' I glared at them. *Well come on, out with it. Let's hear the worst.*

Fred looked from me to Wright to Julie to my mother, fiddling with his lunchbox and *aheming* nervously in his throat. I was further crushed to learn that I wouldn't be allowed home that weekend. I cried. I begged. They didn't budge an inch. All I wanted now was to get out of there. I had tasted the reality of the place and it was bad.

'What if I've put on a pound by tomorrow?' I snivelled, wiping my face with my hands. 'That's the requirement for leave . . .'

'Well, you won't have,' said the dietician, more gently than Wright. I wondered how she could give me a certainty now.

Mum wanted me to come home for the weekend too; but they were having none of it.

'Can't you take me anyway?' I begged afterwards, still sobbing. 'Take me away from this.'

'I can't,' she said desperately. 'I signed the papers, Jessica; I agreed to put you in their care.'

Before I went to bed, I felt cold and hard again. I messed and fiddled with my supper, eating part, slipping part into the bin concealed in a piece of tissue. The voice of the Monkey was calling: '*You've eaten too much, you fat pig. You'll have put on too much weight.*'

But to my vast surprise, I felt a tiny inkling of

something deep inside my stomach as I lay in bed that night. It was a strange feeling, so distant as to be almost forgotten; as though a teeny tiny worm were gnawing in my guts, deep down. I was hungry! Well, not hungry, but just slightly peckish. I'd had practically everything on that gargantuan meal plan. But when I'd been eating almost nothing, I had felt full up with rocks!

I now know that this is a common phenomenon. You can train a starving body to be immune to hunger; then, once you start to eat again, the normal appetite begins to reawaken. Some anorexics feel ravenous once they start to eat. Then they are terrified that they'll never be able to stop again. But at that moment I was just astonished.

Don't be ridiculous! I rebuked my stomach silently. *Use some of the billions of calories I gave you!*

I went to sleep, and in the morning I had lost another half-pound.

chapter four

Saturday. The unit was quiet and still for the weekend. Most people had gone home. On Friday I had eaten everything, but on Saturday I started refusing again, racked with a deep guilt and grief. I was thinking of my father once more. In the afternoon I was allowed out because the nurse on duty didn't know the rules. My mum took me to visit his grave. The sky was pale. The air was still cold, the trees mostly bare, but the first buds were beginning to poke tentative fingers out over the end of the branches. There were hardly any people about. I breathed free air and stood over the grave, saying, 'I'm sorry, I'm sorry, I'm sorry,' about a hundred times.

What would he think of me now? Nothing good. Nothing worth being proud of. My dad was very strong inside and very calm and very very giving. When I was small, I wanted more than anything to be like him: to command that kind of love and respect without ever raising my voice. When he was proud of me, my world lit up. When he taught me things, they were wise. When people said I took after my father, it was the greatest compliment I could've hoped for.

But I'm not like that, I thought suddenly. *I have nothing like that kind of dignity. I had more dignity before.*

My dad loved creativity, and he loved to see me create. He read my childish scribblings with great attention, praised me and talked to me as though I'd be a writer. One day my brother and I were drawing pictures, and I said, 'I'd like to draw a clock.'

With my dad's help, I not only drew a clock, but made an actual working clock out of a cardboard pizza base, which we hung on my bedroom wall. I remember the sense of pride, of awe, holding my (partial) creation in my hands and thinking, *I made this.* What was I making now? Nothing. I was destroying; the force that was supposed to drive my life inverted, warped and twisted by the Monkey.

I still did not eat very much that day, and I wasn't even listening to the Monkey. I was just sad, and tears were choking my throat, leaving no space for food to go down. But when my mum came in the evening (she could be with me more often at the weekend), she was upset that I'd refused a sandwich at tea; so I went back and ate it. Not just any sandwiches. High-calorie, pre-packed hospital sandwiches, filled chock-a-block with cheese. The three sins anorexics fear most are chocolate, chips and cheese, and cheese is the gravest of these. They call them the three Cs. Some of the girls made their own sandwiches, with low-fat sandwich meat brought in from home. I was not allowed to do that, because my weight was so low the staff thought I might contract some bacteria from outside food that I wouldn't be able to fight.

So I was eating again, but only because I didn't want to hurt my mother any more than I already had. There was nothing in me, yet, that thought I'd better do it for myself. I didn't feel that I needed it to live; it was just compliance. But compliance is better than nothing, and slowly, slowly, as sanctions were revoked and the Troll had less excuse to persecute me, unit life became more bearable.

I didn't cry so much any more. I began to feel stronger inside. Because I was eating, I was thinking clearly, and I could write again. Moreover, I felt like writing. I played a sort of game in unit school with Janet. She had these flash cards, and on each one was a short phrase like 'green ball' or 'brown box', and she would give me each one as the title for a poem. I ought to have been doing schoolwork, but who cared? I was alive again. I was literally coming back to life. I was putting food into my body, and I could feel the blood course through my veins again, and my head felt bright and alert. My nerves tingled and my muscles stretched. I still looked emaciated – not in my own head; I've seen photographs – but I felt alive again, and I could write. Janet loved the poems. I flushed and smiled with the pleasure of the artist and the egotist. I'd forgotten how much I enjoyed that feeling.

chapter five

I got a card from my class at school. That was a shock: I'd thought my class despised me. I knew Rachel had set it up because the card had a dolphin on the front, and she had a thing about dolphins. Pretty much the whole class – and a few more – wrote me messages inside. In many styles of handwriting with many pens:

To Jess Hope you get well soon lots of love Tina

Hey Jessi we all miss u like mad! So get well soon! (U soon! Luv Katie A

Hi Jess get well and come back soon Jon

Yo Jess get well soon cos everyone misses you loads Fiona.

To Jessica Get better soon you're missin all the fun at school! (not!) LUV Laura

Hey Jessi How u doing? Missin u loads come back soon Luv Joanne

Missed me? Love? That meant – could it mean – they had valued me? Despite how horrible and nasty I'd become, at-one time people had liked me! Their messages looked so sweet and sincere, set out all over the pages. Even the teacher wrote to me. I had a nice form teacher, Mr Smith, and he'd been saying for a long time that I could always talk to him if anything was wrong. But I couldn't talk in those days because I didn't understand it. The longer messages were mostly from the girls; the boys wrote '*Get well soon luv [name]*', but it didn't matter. The effort said more than anything else. So before I could reconsider, I went out into the corridor and phoned Rachel.

'If I put on a pound by Thursday I can come home for the weekend,' I told Rachel.

To her the answer was simple: 'Eat loads then!' I winced, but just said I would try to do that. I didn't want to say too much about the unit and upset her. She was a lovely girl, innocent, non-malicious and accepting. I know she found me exciting: because I had drive and felt passionately about things, I brought new experiences to her. But she could never understand this place, or share this experience even second-hand, and I did not want her to.

chapter six

Thursday. Weigh day. I had put on 0.1 of a kilo. Not nearly enough to go home. Natural reserve went bye-bye. I cried. I wept. I begged for weekend leave. I went from the therapist to the psychiatrist's office, literally got down on my knees.

'Ask Doctor Wright for me,' I pleaded with Louise, my therapist. I still saw her twice a week and had still told her nothing. 'Ask her to let me go home.'

'Well no, I won't,' Louise said, looking terribly uncomfortable.

'Why?'

'You haven't put the weight on.'

'Well that's *not my fault!*'

Dubious. I was 'adhering to the meal plan', as they put it (to this day I retain an unceasing hatred of the word 'adhere'); but with the little nips and tucks all anorexics make. Shaking crumbly bits off cereal, under-measuring juice and milk, smearing and scraping food

around plates. I was supposed to get four small potatoes with my lunch and took three – nobody checked
things like that. In the end, I think Louise did something, as they conceded that I could have Monday night
at home, if I put on a pound by then. Well, I did put
the pound on and I was allowed to go home.

Our house seemed like heaven – I hugged the couch.
My brother and my mum and I played Scrabble – I
won – then we watched television together and we
laughed. My brother, Adam, seemed really glad to have
me home and I was touched. I suppose he thought I
was going to get better now, and then things would
be OK.

When it came to supper, I froze in the middle of my
biscuit. 'Somebody say something encouraging!' I was
caught between tears and laughter.

'No,' said Mum, 'because you have to do this for
yourself.'

For myself? Unthinkable: I didn't deserve food! I had
to know somebody else wanted me to eat . . .

'Go on, Jess,' said Adam in his kindest voice, so I
seized that and ate it for his sake. I stayed up very late,
trying to stretch the night out as long as possible, but
of course Tuesday morning came all too soon, and it
was straight back to the unit.

But at last I had begun to gain weight, and life at the unit had become a little better. For a start, each day my mum came in to visit me, and as I was 'adhering', we were sometimes allowed as much as two hours together. We sat in a small room by ourselves when we could get it, and talked, and played Scrabble. I needed constant reassurance:

'Am I fat? Am I getting fat yet?'

My mum would make me lift my shirt up and count all the ribs, which I could still see, and the prominent knobs down my spine. She made me observe myself in the reflective glass and tell her what I saw.

'I look OK,' I said.

'You look,' she said flatly, 'like an anorexic. You have always been a very pretty girl, Jessica, but for the first time in your life you've made yourself quite ugly.'

I often had weekend leave now. The first time I just stayed at home, rejoicing. The second I ventured out to the shops, and when I got back Rachel and Joanne were there waiting for me. We met with hugs and exclamations. I took them up to my room.

'I'm so glad to see you guys!' I cried.

'We're . . . glad to see you too, Jess,' said Rachel. She did not look very glad. In fact she looked sort of

172

horrified, perching on my bed, scrutinizing my body and face and attempting to look like she wasn't.

You should've seen me at my lowest weight, I wanted to say. *You should've seen how far I went with this, how I proved everyone wrong.* Instead I asked, 'How's school?'

'Shit,' said Joanne. 'Er, Michael O'Brien water-bombed Mr Matthews's PE class. That's the biggest news of the month. Also, the physics student cried and Mr Lowry is retiring. How's—?'

'The unit's shit too,' and we giggled.

There was a long pause. Then Joanne said, 'What's it like? I mean, what do you do all day?'

'Well, I . . . go to school. I don't get a holiday or anything. I still have to do work.' I suddenly felt it important to tell them this – *I have nothing whatsoever to envy.* 'And I see therapists and shit. They don't help.'

'Why did you do it, Jess?' Rachel burst out suddenly, hands tightening on the bedclothes, looking as though she wanted to spring out of her seat. 'Was it because people bullied you? Said you were fat?'

I closed my eyes briefly. *Why did you do it, Jess? Oh God, I can't begin to tell you. I don't know why I did it. I did it for control. Because the world is crazy. Because I learned too young that everything is unstable and shaky and false and the only way to get any certainty is to goddamn make it yourself . . .*

173

Because I miss Dad. Because madness is chemical and hered-
itary – and look at my grandmother. Because I was bored. Oh
God. I don't know, I don't know why I did it – because there's
a monkey in my head!

'Yes,' I told her. 'Partly it was because people bullied
me.'

On the surface, it was as though I'd never been away.
But underneath, everything was different. I was truly
grateful that they'd come and glad to see them. But I
felt so . . . old. Detached. I could not tell them much
about the unit. Although nobody's teenage years are
exactly idyllic, it struck me very sharply that my friends
simply would not believe some of the things I had seen.
I knew then that I was neither the troubled girl who'd
scared the hell out of them before the Christmas break,
nor the person they had known before then. Of course,
we were all changing. Joanne was sitting normally in
my rocking chair and fiddling with a pencil, whereas a
year before she used to jump it up and down so hard
I worried it would crash right through the floorboards.
But I was not just changing. I was undergoing some
kind of metamorphosis, and an incredibly painful one,
as painful as if I were being born all over again.

chapter seven

I went back to the unit on Monday, feeling a little more reconciled to it. I was getting pretty close to Chloe and Bethany, and I looked forward to seeing them. But this was no happy teenage social club. It was still a psychiatric unit, and at any time a person might break down and cry and scream; we would cry together in the evenings and discuss terrible things.

I got talking to Manda over our Scrabble games. The first time, I was confident I'd win. I usually do at Scrabble, even against adults.

'Do you want to go first?' Manda offered.

'No, you go.'

I thought I could afford to let her have the double-word-score square in the centre that starts the game off. When I begin, I try to get a 'BARN' or 'RICE' – the B or C to boost the score a bit, but obviously nothing fancy as there's only the dealt hand to work with. I studied my letters for a moment while she looked at hers. Then I glanced back at the board. I blinked. In the time I'd dropped my eyes, the word QUIRKY had appeared on the board from Manda's dealt hand, with the Q on a double-letter square. She looked up at me and smiled quietly. Her eye held a glint.

'Er, good move,' I said.

'Thank you,' she answered.

Ah, shit, I thought.

'Do you know,' she asked after roundly kicking my butt, 'why all the plates here are plastic? And the cups, too?'

I shook my head. We were sitting with our backs against the couch now – Sally was in therapy, and Robert was listening to his headphones on the other side of the room.

'It's because of me,' said Manda.

I waited.

'I've tried to kill myself in here. They don't let you have anything sharp, of course.' This was true. They'd taken my nail scissors. 'So I broke a plate when they were china and I cut my wrists on the shards. But they caught me. So I tried to run away and there was a scuffle – and I ducked through Eleanor's arms just as somebody opened the door from the outside. I made a dash for it – but of course they caught me and brought me back here.'

176

I stared at her in horror. Across her little wrists were many slashes, healed over and re-scarred. I couldn't look at them. But then, at other times, she was like any other teenage girl, and would laugh and talk about shopping and dresses. She was generous and giving by nature; the only person I have ever heard speak guarded defence of Eleanor Troll. I could think of nothing to say in response to her story, except lamely, 'I'm sorry.'

'Hardly your fault.' She gave me that old wry smile. Presently Sally came in.

'How was therapy?'

'Boring.' We laughed.

'We talked about the times I was afraid to brush my teeth. I dunno what the point was, really. We did that last week.'

'I was afraid to brush my teeth, too,' I confessed.

'And I was,' said Manda.

'Because of the toothpaste?' I looked from one to the other.

'Of course' – Sally's mouth twitched – 'but you know, I look at you, and I just think, *You're so skinny, Jessica.*'

'And to me, *you're* thin!' *Not to mention beautiful.* She was still as doll-like and lovely as the first time I'd ever glimpsed her, her skin such a perfect white.

'Oh no, I'm not,' she said. 'I'm normal.'

'No, *I'm* normal,' I said.

Manda affirmed this: 'Yes, you look normal to me. You look right. If you don't mind me saying so, you're not as slim as Sally.' Her best friend smiled gratefully and clutched her hand. Manda held onto it.

'Oh no,' I hastened to assure them both. 'I know.'

'But I feel fat,' said Manda.

'No, no, you look very nice,' said Sally hollowly, and they sighed and leaned towards each other.

Thin, *slim* and *skinny* are interchangeable words to anorexics for anything outside the dreaded realm of fatness. Most of the others had photographs – 'Me before it started . . . Me at my lowest weight' – which we would pore over and discuss; the subject staring at his or her 'slimmest weight', longing to have it again.

I still did not say much in therapy with Louise. She had begun to probe me about my family:

'Do you get on with your mother?'

'Yeah.'

'Even now that you're ill?'

'Sometimes we argue.' *Maybe you were born like it . . . Oh so it's my fault!* I briefly closed my eyes.

'Do you wish it was like before, when you didn't argue?'

I cocked an eyebrow insolently. 'We did argue before.'

'But not like now?'

'No. Not like now.'

'So you feel you argue more now that you have the illness. How do you feel about that?'

'Bad.' That was what I was meant to say. It wasn't quite the truth. Sometimes I regretted our arguments, sometimes they filled me with guilt – other times they were refreshing and exorcizing, like the anguished exclamations that had led to making the 'contract'. I did not trust Louise with any of this stuff. I saw her two hours a week, as one of a number of clients. No one to whom I was a number in a file deserved to know these things.

I was lucky not to have Jane Wright, as Sally did. She was very hard, and all acknowledged it.

Eleanor was still a thorn, and still hated me. She took every opportunity to put me down, emphasize my failings and belittle my successes. I did not behave for Eleanor. We had a power struggle going on. One time, a small group of us was sat at the table: me, Manda, Sally and a new, equally thin girl who had appeared that morning. Eleanor had served me up a specially large portion of cake and custard. She looked at me across the table and smirked very pointedly. So I just met her gaze and said, flat as flat, 'I'm not going to eat that.'

I did not even bother to wrangle with the Monkey. I didn't owe *her* any favours, and I only ate in order to please the nurses I liked, to see my mum, and to be allowed home at weekends.

'Yes you are.'

'I *eat* what it says on my meal plan.'

'This *is* on your meal plan, Jessica.'

'It says a pudding. That is not a normal-sized pudding.'

'I say it is.'

'Nobody else would. I know what the others serve me.'

'Well, today *I'm* serving, aren't I?'

'If you try and make me, I'm going to scream.'

'You're not going to scream.'

I have quite a low voice for a girl, but when I want to scream, I really scream, deafeningly loudly. My pitch goes through the roof. Being naturally reserved, I've only done this a handful of times in my life. One summer when I was six and took my bike out for the first time that year before I had checked the brakes. We lived on a hill then with a main road at the bottom, and before I knew it, *whoooooosh*, the brakes had failed, and I was streaming down towards a certain doom – *then* I really screamed. I also screamed after my dad died, alone in my room, but even then I smothered the sound with my pillow. I had to do this because there was a neverending parade of friends and relations coming in and out of the house, bearing flowers, cakes, etc. But this time, holding that squinty pale troll's eye over the top of the table, I just screamed. I didn't know that I was really going to do it till I did. It rebounded off the walls and caused the others to clamp their hands over their ears.

'Oh, for goodness' sake!' shouted Manda angrily amidst the latter part of it, as Sally started sobbing.

I don't know what I did then – cried or ran away – my mind sort of blanked out for a little while. Afterwards I was full of remorse; not a jot for Eleanor, but for the others. The Monkey indulged in '*They hate you, they hate you!*' which as far as the new girl was concerned seemed to be true. Manda and Sally had forgotten by the morning: they had seen far worse. But she eyed me like a pestilence and I loathed myself for it.

Group therapy was hard that day. When people did talk in group they really talked. Completely spilled the beans. That was where I heard some of the stories from the other patients, of their dreadful past lives. There were things that shocked me, things that terrified me, things that made me sob with pity and with guilt for my own selfishness. All right, so my dad had died and my nan had got dementia, but compared to what some of the others had gone through, I had no right to be crazy.

'*But he wasn't just my dad*' – the good voice spoke up adamantly – '*he was my hero and protector and the person I was closest to in the world. We did everything together. I was Daddy's girl through and through.*'

'*Nonetheless,*' the Monkey jeered, '*you should've been stronger. Other people have coped with worse and not cracked up.*'

Why, why was I so weak to be like this?

In group therapy I heard the sort of things that, when you read about them in the paper, make you gasp and tut and say, 'What are we coming to? How *terrible*. How awful for the *children*.' And then you close the paper and forget all about them again. Only these were people I knew well and cared about, and they were telling me the truth, so I couldn't just forget about it afterwards. One person told; and then another told; and pretty soon we were all talking and crying for the world and for each other.

People cry in different ways. Some loudly, holding hands or hugging the person next to them. Some quiet, muffled, curled into a ball. Some just sit there, staring into space, as tears trickle down their cheeks, and their eyes are haunted. It was a purgative. Afterwards the girls hugged and cried in the corridor. The boys sprinted for their dorms. Then we sort of felt better – no, not better, but cleaned out to some degree. Part purged. And exhausted.

chapter eight

'I used to be a heroin addict.'

'Did you?' I turned to Bethany with wide eyes.

We were standing outside after tea one day, taking some air. Well, I was taking air; she was taking cigarette smoke, but, hey – better than heroin. Almost everybody at the unit smoked, including many of the nurses. Some heavily; some, like Chloe and Manda, just now and then to calm down.

We stood out on the closest thing the unit had to a garden, which was a little paved space beyond the community-room doors. There was a low wall, which we used to sit on, and a basketball hoop without any net. It's not like exercise was discouraged. On the contrary: three times a week, the kids who did not have an eating disorder would be taken over to the 'gym', which I suppose was in the main part of the hospital. They were actively urged to go by their nurses, as exercise brings relief from depression. Even those with eating disorders, so long as they continued to gain sufficient weight, were encouraged to exercise.

'What's it like?' I said to Bethany. 'The heroin, I mean.' The afternoon was fading, and the pallid winter sun went down before us in a faint thumb-smudge of orange. The sky was quite light.

'Bad,' she said. 'It's bad shit. That's why I cut deep, that one time when I got admitted here. Before, I made it sound like an accident, but—'

'I know.' Not about drugs specifically, but I knew. I was used to the look of her arms now, but I still hated them. She offered me her cigarette.

'I don't smoke.'

'Nice one.'

Bethany's mobile rang. She glanced at me apologetically, conscious of its jarring sound against the pale cool air, and fished it out of her handbag. She did not answer it. First she pressed a button, then she looked at the screen.

'My stepfather.' A brief look of distress and distaste crossed her features. 'He knows – he *knows* he's not meant to . . .'

Contact her, I finished mentally. I thought of various reasons why that could be and didn't like any of them. I looked out at the skyline, unable to meet her eyes, and thought about what a lovely, sweet person she was and how much I liked and admired her. *Not fair. Not fair.*

After a pause the mobile rang again.

'Why don't you turn it off?' I suggested.

'Nah.' She grinned, a little embarrassed. 'It might be Robert.' Robert was out on leave.

'When did you meet Robert?' This seemed like safer territory.

'Oh, two years ago.' She grinned again.

'And where?'

'Here.'

I winced. Two years was a long time to imagine being around this place. Still, I guess I should've seen that coming. As though she'd read my mind, she slid her eyes over. 'It's not an overnight thing, sweetie. Getting better.'

'No.'

'Rob's so great, though, he's . . . he understands. I can't imagine being with someone now who hadn't been through it. He makes me laugh,' and then in appeal to me: 'That's got to be good, hasn't it?'

I knew what she was getting at. None of the nurses would comment on Robert and Bethany; but a raised eyebrow, a dry look – it was enough for suggestion. *A dangerous bond?* they were wondering. *Two people, so close, with that shared vice?*

'The one good thing I have left,' my friend cried suddenly, and crushed her cigarette out on the wall. 'The one good, pure thing – and they look down on it. As though it were cheap or dirty.'

'It isn't,' I said.

'No. But drugs are.' Her mouth twitched as she added this, drily, as though she had suddenly remembered she was older than me and ought to give responsible advice. I studied the piece of wall moss I was picking at.

The only drugs I took were on prescription. Prozac had been a miserable failure, so now they had put me on Seroxat. I found it better. This was years ago, before all the controversy over that drug, which is mostly tabloid hype. Even so, they don't usually give it to under-eighteens any more because of the suicide rate. It's a bastard to get off, too, but it seemed to be working for me. I also took a pill to go to sleep. Up, down, up, down. Like a ping-pong ball. All the drugs were kept in a chest in the cold clinic room, and every night a senior nurse unlocked it and doled out the miracles in little cups.

We leaned on the wall in amiable silence for a little while, watching the sun bleed and die. Presently we heard a noise behind us. Chloe, Manda and Sally had appeared with a nurse.

'Scream therapy,' Manda said.

'What's scream therapy?'

I soon learned. We all stood in a circle, holding hands. The nurse, a large, placid woman of middling years, joined us. Dusk was falling fast, and the eyes and teeth of my companions gleamed dully in the gloom. The air tingled.

'Ready?' asked Manda. All nodded. 'Now.' Then the group drew in a collective breath, and suddenly I knew what was coming. The sound was ear-splitting. As we were girls, the scream was piercing and high-pitched, gashing the still air like arrows. Even the nurse was screaming. We screamed until our breath gave out, and then we drew in breath and screamed a second time, and then a third. When it was over I was gasping.

'Releases all your tension,' Chloe panted.

'Mm.' Nods, smiles. I agreed. Not quite as satisfying as the time I screamed in Eleanor's face – now that had been scream therapy.

Then across the field someone shouted, 'Shut the *fuck* up! People are trying to sleep!'

'What the hell you sleeping in a field for?' I bellowed back. Manda laughed wholeheartedly; I glowed. Now that I knew about her I was more in awe than ever. A nobility and fascination is born of extreme suffering. I think we are all voyeurs at heart.

chapter nine

Into this came Luke.

'Have you heard about the new boy?' asked Manda, raising her eyebrows. A group of us were at a table in the creative room, painting designs on fabric. It was supposed to be relaxing; and I took a guilty pleasure in it, doing primary-school activity at an hour when once I'd have been doing physics.

'I've heard that someone's coming,' Sally said.

'I heard he'll be here by lunch time,' said Robert.

'He *is* here,' said Manda. 'I've seen him. Being shown about for the first time.' We raised our eyebrows at each other.

'What's he like?' said another girl eagerly. 'Is he, you know, good looking?'

'Mm.' Manda exchanged a pointed look with Sally. She made the tilt-hand gesture for 'OK'.

I did not see him till mid-afternoon, first a glimpse in passing in the dining room, then wandering about the corridor. He was tall, maybe five foot eleven or six foot, and definitely did not weigh more than I did. Probably less. I suppose I would guess six stone. I've seen those nightmare photos from the Holocaust. Concentration-camp-starved bodies piled in pits. The face of a starving man, empty eyes hollowed, tired. Now I met a person who had done that to himself. Was still doing it.

He was walking about. Even the bones in his face showed. He was wearing trousers and a jumper so I could not see the full extent of his emaciation. But then in the evening he wore football shorts to supper. His legs were literally skin and bone. That expression is used far too often. The reality of it is morbid. When I saw them I felt sort of sick again. He sat down at the table, which was laid with biscuits, tea, hot chocolate, Weetabix, All Bran and fruit. Luke smiled and nodded to everyone – he had the manners of an old-time gentleman – then sat down at the table. He poured a cup of tea and dribbled milk in. I watched the way he poured the milk, so carefully, carefully, scrutinizing every drop to make sure he did not pour too much. His hand shook very slightly. My heart actually ached.

He was quiet, but painstakingly polite. He had been talking with Robert about football, which was nice. Boys always talk about football in happy, normal situations. But, oh God, he just looked so terrible. If someone needed something, he would jump up to go and get it. A napkin, spoon or fork. He put the chairs away and got them out. He could not stop moving, could not sit down for a moment. Sometimes he just paced up and down the room.

'That boy's going to wear a hole in the carpet,' Pip remarked.

Argh, I wished someone would stop him. But what could you do? It was his first day at the unit; he had no bed there yet. He had not been sectioned, he was still upright and coherent, somehow – more coherent than I had been. He wasn't crying; he was calm and collected and pleasant. His parents cried though. My mother saw them in the foyer.

'The looks on their faces,' she said afterwards, quietly. 'Of such . . . desperation. Confusion.'

I wanted to talk to Luke. Not to say anything deep. Just to speak with him. It was partly the fascinated awe with which we view extremes of suffering, partly pity and sorrow. After supper he was standing (not sitting) by the wall of the serving hatch, where our meal plans were pinned for the servers. He read them silently, his haggard face impassive.

'Yep, those are the meal plans,' I said conversation-ally. 'And when I first saw mine, I cried.'

He looked across at me and smiled. It seemed a strange expression on those wasted features.

'I'm Jessica,' I offered.

'Luke.' We shook hands. Carefully.

'I don't like to say welcome or anything. I mean, it's pretty shit here.' I laughed helplessly. 'So. Er – what kind of stuff – do you like?'

'Football.' He smiled. 'I'd love to go professional. I play for a semi-pro team already. Played,' he corrected himself.

'That's great,' I said. 'I mean, great that you did. Not – not great that you had to stop. You will play again, I'm sure . . .' *Anytime would be a good time to stop talking, Jessica . . .*

'What kind of stuff do *you* like?' He saved me.

'Well, reading. And writing. All kinds of music . . .' Pause. My heart was beating extremely fast in my chest, partly that fear-awe again, partly the fact I was standing here, holding a conversation with a boy with green eyes and beautiful manners. *And a Body Mass Index of ten.* He looked, in a word, disgusting – but he was a boy, being kind to me, and this was a lonely place.

* * *

192

Most people went to bed about eleven, and gathered in the community room beforehand. They played pool and music, almost like a teenage club. But you could never lose that sense of desperation underneath, the *I don't want to be here, let me go*, the haunted looks in people's eyes. Unexpected things happened suddenly. That night a boy named Joshua jumped up and grabbed the whiteboard pen.

'My mum is A-slash-B!' he called out loudly, scrawling it across the board. 'Anorexic-*slash*-bulimic!'

I jumped a mile. Joshua was usually very placid, very kind, and *never* spoke about himself. He had cried with the rest of us that time in group therapy, but revealed nothing. I assumed he self-harmed, because he always wore long sleeves. The room was very quiet, the air suddenly heavy. I wondered what it would feel like, to have an anorexic parent.

That woman must be even more selfish than I am, I thought darkly. *Doing that to her child and all. If I ever have children, I'll be a good mother to them. I will. I'll put their needs before my own, even, even—*

'*How will you?*' the Monkey asked. '*You'll just screw it up. You could never be a mother without ruining the children's lives.*'

Oh, shut it. I'm so tired.

Supper time was a bad time. A terrible thing. I saw another of those things that will be emblazoned on my mind for ever. Manda stood up suddenly and started screaming, smashed a china plate that had somehow found its way onto the table and tried to slit her wrists with it. Sally screamed as well; Luke sprang up with lightning-like reactions and held her in place. '*He's strong, he's in control,*' admired the Monkey.

Nurses leaped to restrain Manda. I froze in terror and watched the sick scene unfold. *I want to go home, I want to go home!* my mind screamed. *Let me out of here! I don't want to be like this, don't want to grow up and be Joshua's mum* . . .

A girl buried her face in her hands. People screamed and wailed. The sound dwindled to the stunned clink of cutlery and Manda's ragged sobbing. The smashed plate was all on the floor. Eleanor told everyone to leave the table. We moved fast.

Sally didn't take Luke's actions amiss. She liked him. And he liked her back. We had all seen them talking together with heads bent, hands just close enough for suggestion, tones hushed. Once I saw her hand in his and it looked strange – I was so used to seeing it in Manda's.

That night I sobbed to my mum, 'Please, please take

194

me out of here! It's too awful! Too scary!' The longer I stayed here, the further I got from life. I could feel it happen: a new life was forming here, a cut-off, bad life, but a life that day to day was manageable. I could just imagine, fearfully, how a day would come when the doors of the unit would be thrown wide open. I would contemplate them, look out at street and sky, then shake my head and shrink back inside. I've heard of people who stay in mental institutions their whole life. I was starting to see how it happened and it terrified me. I did not want to be one of those people. I wanted out; I wanted out now.

But it was not up to me – the papers were signed, the doors locked, and the guard-nurses prowled the corridors.

All around me were frightening things. Luke, for one. He could not go on like that much longer. I actually saw him being sectioned. Mum and I were sitting in the reception during visiting hours, as the private rooms were all in use. Then we suddenly heard a muffled shout, a smash and clink of glass. Suicide attempts seemed to be catching. A moment later, Luke was led out – literally led – before our eyes, supported by two male nurses, and the expression of *defeat*, of total, final, ultimate despair in his face struck me like a thunderbolt. His hollowed eyes said, *It's over. Do what you will. I can't keep fighting any more.* But whether he was saying this to the illness or the carers I could not say. His parents followed at the back of that grim procession, expressions of utter confusion and pain on their faces.

They were taking him over to the main part of the hospital, to be fed by a tube up his nose. All power to make decisions was taken from him and his parents. This is sectioning under the Mental Health Act, the cruellest and kindest extent of the service's power.

The Monkey was completely silent as I watched Luke being sectioned. No amount of twisting or distorting could make something good or enviable out of that scene. The silence where I had become accustomed to the guidance of its voice was shocking: exhilaration and fear.

Luke, who could have been a footballer. Manda, who could have been anything she wanted. *They still could!* I told myself. *And me? Could I?* I had learned there is a certain type of person whose most powerful enemy is within themselves, more than capable of snuffing out their life. The deepest, darkest, most destructive facet of the person has an opposite that, when allowed, shines bright and clear and powerful. In very basic language, the artistic temperament. There is a Hindu god called

196

Hanuman. He is both creator and destroyer. Hanuman destroys the old and useless and regenerates new life. Luckily he doesn't get it backwards. In so many ways these opposites are linked. If a creative and achievement-driven person, for whatever reason, stops creating and achieving, his or her fire will turn to destruction. Interestingly, Hanuman is a monkey.

chapter ten

Chloe and I were making a newspaper. Well, all right, Chloe did most of the real work. We both liked writing, and we wrote and drew, and we collected pictures, stories, poetry and puzzles from the others in the unit. Manda went out one night to a drama group and wrote up her experience. Sally wrote a poem with a line or two on every person in the unit, which ended by praising all of us as stars. Janet was our main supporter in putting the paper together, and she let us spend a lot of lesson time on it. We typed the stuff up on computer, then got every patient at the unit, even those who did not contribute, to draw a little picture of themselves, which we stuck on the back. The paper didn't look professional, but it looked all right, and most importantly we'd made it ourselves. We had created something for a change, rather than destroying.

Chloe and I talked while we worked. Sometimes about ordinary things, sometimes about our problems. I had seen her problems: scratches, scars all up her arms, even one on her cheek. One afternoon she and I were in Janet's classroom, busy with the newspaper. I was on a stool, and she was kneeling on the floor nearby cutting out little pictures. I was surprised to see her handling the scissors because she didn't like blades and things. A few days previously, at the table, I had been sitting toying with my fork; completely absent-mindedly, I ran the tines along my fingers, prodding them gently.

'Please don't do that,' Chloe whispered. I looked up, and to my shock I saw her staring at me, frozen, with a stricken, haunted look in her dark eyes. I quickly put the fork down, and was careful not to handle anything sharp like that again in her presence. But now she knelt and snipped away quite calmly, scissor points facing away.

'Do you think of it as a monkey?' I was saying. 'That's what Jane Wright says.'

'Oh, her. Well, no – more of a voice. A male voice.'

'Really? It's female with me. Or I think it is. In fact I'm pretty sure it's *my* voice.'

'No, with me it's definitely a man. He tempts me to do things; bad things. He says I look more beautiful with scratches.'

'How strange.' The Monkey thought I was more

beautiful when I was thin, but that's a common stereotype. I had never seen scratches and scars held up as beautiful. At least not overtly. *Shit, if any company did, the Advertising Standards Authority would be down on them like a ton of bricks. I wonder why it's not the same with thinness?*

I would not call Chloe fat, not even in my own head, but she was a big girl and quite chunky. She was always on and off a reducing diet that Julie had written out for her, and the results were beginning to show. We congratulated her enviously when she lost weight, craving the buzz like crack. I was eating – it seemed copious amounts – and my weight was hovering; up a bit, then down a little, then stay the same . . . but the trend was a snail's pace upwards, and the dreaded figure of seven stone was approaching. I had made a deal with my mum that I would worry about that when I got there. The dietician would still not give me a target weight, but I had a suspicion they'd said something to my mum, and I ordered her to tell me right away if I was even approaching it.

But Chloe had no issues about weight loss, none whatsoever. She was not even that disciplined a dieter. Once, after finishing the low-fat meal on her diet, she sat there, musing, and grinned. 'Oh, Pip, I'm going to have the pudding.'

And that was fine – no guilt, as far as I know. Overall, she must have been good enough, because the weight came off her. *God*, I remember thinking when I watched her, *if I could just do that – I wouldn't even be here.* But then I dare say Chloe thought along similar lines, seeing me toy with a fork.

chapter eleven

Valentine's Day makes me gag. Maybe you have to be in love to appreciate it, but to me the teenybopper shrieks and giggles that punctuate it from the time you reach the age of nine just wreck the sentiment.

In the first and second years of high school it was awful. Being such a needy child, I idolized people at random and developed a crush every time a boy ignored my fat. If he had a kind word and a joke for me I adored him.

Then Valentine's Day would come, and I wouldn't get cards, and my little group and I would saunter round pretending to scorn romance, shouting, 'Get a room!' at busy couples. We were hurting inside because we felt so backward, wondering what it would be like to have a boy's hands on our bodies, at the same time shivering and thanking our lucky stars that we didn't.

Valentine's Day at the unit was something different altogether.

People started to mention it about two weeks in advance. Every minor holiday was an event there, because people's lives were so dreary. The girls started talking of shopping for dresses, when they went home for the weekend.

'I know just the one I want,' said Chloe wistfully.

'I'm not sure yet,' said Manda. 'When I see the one that speaks to me, I'll know.' She smiled and closed her eyes; her lips trembled – I thought half in laughter, half in desperation at the futility of it all.

'I wonder if Luke will be back for the party,' said Sally.

Luke had come back once already from the main part of the hospital, a tube taped to his face and leading up his nose. The other end was not connected to anything – I guess they hooked it up intermittently. But he could not keep still, and a junior or student nurse said he could walk to the shops. Two paces out of the door, he'd collapsed and been taken straight back to the hospital.

I asked what the party was like.

'Oh, music, food, you know, usual things.'

'Food?' I said dubiously.

'For the others,' Manda reassured me, meaning the non-anorexics.

'I hope he comes back,' said Sally quietly, and traced the tabletop with her finger. I felt a frown crease my features. Sally really liked him. And *of course* he liked her back – she was *beautiful*, and thin and full of sweetness. Dammit. I conjured up the image of Luke's green eyes, the gravelly sound of his voice, the aura of nobility he'd earned for taking this further than any of us, for being the hardest, the strongest. This was bizarre. In the Other World, the Outside, the only reason I'd have looked twice at Luke would be to stare in horror. Well, this wasn't the Outside, was it?

'Who'll be with who at the party?' we asked each other jokingly, and Manda took it upon herself to arrange this. One day I went into the community room to find her and Sally drawing hearts on the whiteboard, and filling them in with people's names in boy-girl pairs. Obviously Bethany and Robert were paired together, and Manda herself claimed the quiet, unassuming Joshua, who was easily the best-looking boy.

Sally got Luke. Figures: her best friend made the pairings.

I told myself not to be an idiot. As if I could handle any kind of relationship anyway, leave alone one with him. The question was whether I could handle seeing him and beautiful thin Sally together. Well, shit happens.

Underneath the pairings, Manda had written the date of the party and:

Girls must wear dresses.
Boys - smart trousers (no jeans!).

'The pairings are just to exchange cards,' she explained. 'So nobody's left out.' I scanned the board for my name and saw it paired with a tall, placid boy named Damian. He never said much, moved slowly and had pale, wide eyes. He reminded me of a powerful animal, drugged – then someone whispered that he suffered from schizophrenia, and had once been dangerously violent. After that I tried to get the drugged-animal image out of my head. It clung.

I blinked. I couldn't really see him coming to the party; he usually hid himself away in his room, except for meals. And to use the phone. The phone was a source of contention because everybody always wanted to use it, as a link to the outside world, but our time on it was rationed and shared out between us. Phone calls could be barred as punishment for bad behaviour, like in prison.

So Damian was my Valentine, at least where cards were concerned. I'd never had a Valentine before. Part of me wished that it could mean more than cards; that maybe this would open up some friendship or some confidence. Would it be possible to converse with Damian, or would the medication . . . ? I shivered.

'*Moot point,*' the Monkey advised me. '*He'd never want to be friends with a stupid cow like you anyway.*'

'*I could at least give it a go.*'

'*Your time to waste. Just don't come crying to me when you get shot down. Loser.*'

I did not approach Damian yet, but bought a nondescript card from the village shop, expecting nothing in return.

My mother was pleased about the coming party. She saw it as a positive idea. That week I gained my pound, so she took me into town on Saturday to look at dresses. I was muffled up like an Eskimo against the cold, and peered out from under my hat in the main shopping street. My nose and fingers turned red. The bustling outside world felt alien. People hurrying back and forth in bright-coloured blurs seemed faceless, depthless, unfathomably free. I had little interest in pretty dresses. I related to my mum what Manda had said about knowing her dress when she saw it.

'Yes, it's like that sometimes,' Mum enthused. 'With shopping, something just leaps out at you . . .'

I smiled for her sake and let her chatter. I loved her fiercely for trying so hard to make this a normal shopping trip, a mother-and-daughter town excursion like we used to do. But inside I felt grey. Everything was flat and empty; the world was like a picture painted on a screen for a film studio, but I had looked behind the screen and seen it propped up from behind with crude wooden beams; the space was dim and ugly and disordered. Dresses flitted by and I made arbitrary comments on them. Eventually we found one that Mum liked a lot and I didn't have any objection to: it was pink and flowery and clingy with a ruffle, but a pink too strong to be sickly. We took size eight.

'Does it look nice?' I asked in the changing room.

'Lovely,' said my mother. 'Except you look like a skeleton in it.'

What's she on about? I thought. *It's tight.* And it was. The material was stretchy and it clung to my top half, though you could see the outline of my ribs. *So I'm not thin,* I thought with disappointment. *Size eight is too tight. So I'm not a size eight. I'm not even the smallest size. And they call me thin!* I thought that my legs looked all right, though: the skirt being long, you couldn't see too much of the disgusting curves of thigh and hip that were beginning to sneak back and so embarrassed me. '*Gross,*' snorted the Monkey. '*Weakling. Just look what you're letting them do to you.*'

'*But what choice do I have?*' I countered desperately. '*They can lock me away, not let me see my family . . .*'

'*Weak bitch,*' observed the Monkey. '*No control.*'

'Let's take it,' I said, very loudly in order to cover the dialogue in my head – loud enough and falsely enough to draw the curious glances of some normal shoppers, who raised eyebrows at my appearance.

On the morning of the fourteenth I was woken by a strange, soft noise. At first I thought it was part of my dream.

'*Beep-beep-beep beeeep beeep – Beep-beep-beep beeeep beeep – Beep-beep . . .*' It sounded like somebody's mobile was playing 'You Are My Sunshine' with a monophonic ring tone.

'What the—?'

A second later there came a knock at the door.

'Jess!' It was Sally's voice. I sprang up, adjusted my pyjamas and opened the door. There stood Sally on her own, fully dressed and smiling shyly. In one hand she held a pile of cards, in the other a bouquet of life-size plastic roses, with little heart-shaped red bulbs in their middle. Sally held a flower out to me and pressed a button in the stem. The bulb lit up:

'*Beep-beep-beep beeeep beeep* . . .' and the music played again. I burst out laughing. Sally was going from room to room, handing out the flowers, and a card with a silly poem inside. They were unsigned but I recognized the writing of a staff nurse. I put my card and flower on the cupboard top (my only surface) and got dressed in my Valentine's clothes. I put make-up on, something I hadn't bothered with for a long time, and I left my hair down. I had washed it the previous night; we had to take turns with the showers, but mine had been well timed that week. I felt better with my hair down.

You look normal, I thought, looking in the mirror. *Not too fat – but not slim either. Like an ordinary girl.*

Strained cheerfulness crackled like cellophane at breakfast. Some of the girls had dressed early, like me; others planned to change later. The boys had jeans and jumpers on as always. We anorexics all behaved and ate our food. Nobody screamed or cried. I wondered how I should give Damian his card. As soon as the meal was over he got up and shambled off with his eyes down like he always did.

Mid-morning Luke came back again. So far as I could see he looked no better, but at least he could walk again. Poignantly, he retained his calm, polite, upper-middle-class exterior, ignoring the pathetic piece of tubing still stuck to his cheek and nose, and the heart-rending indignities we'd all witnessed over the past few days. Of course nobody said a thing about them. We welcomed him back like he'd been home for the weekend. No one asked about the hospital. My heart hurt to look at him – I allowed myself to blend the lines between pity, fascination and a crush until they disappeared.

The party was supposed to start at four. I didn't see Damian all day, except once in the foyer, talking with his parents. *Well, kid, it's now or never.* So I got up, tapped him on the shoulder and handed him his card. He looked utterly surprised and mumbled some vague thanks. I just shrugged and smiled and went away again. He didn't want to talk. I was not expecting anything, but in the afternoon, when I went back to my room, I found a new card waiting for me. It was a fairly standard Valentinish deal: brown teddy bear on the front, soppy eyes, with a big red heart in the corner. I opened it, eager and curious. On the inside was simply:

To Jessica
Happy Valentine's Day
From Guess Who?

The writing was large and childish. *Who indeed?* I mused as I carefully closed the card and put it to stand by the first one. I was glad at least that I hadn't offended or angered Damian. Maybe the gesture even pleased him in some way.

He did not come to the party, but it didn't matter, so far as partners were concerned, because hardly anybody danced in pairs. Bethany and Robert did. A little. So did Sally and Luke. A lot. I guess they thought they had a lot of calories to burn. I made myself not watch. Manda's plans were thwarted, as the boys did not dress up. I doubt they even noticed that the girls had, but that was hardly the point. The girls had enjoyed putting on make-up; we had pretended that we were normal carefree teenagers, with no more worries than what colour lipstick matched our skin tones. Bethany did not dress up that much. I guess she didn't feel the need. I always thought she was beautiful anyway.

The party was in the community room. They'd pushed the pool table back across one end and covered it with a cloth for the food. The hospital had sent over some treats: sausage rolls and sandwiches, cakes and chocolates. Crisps in little bowls. The works. Bethany and Chloe hummed and ha'ed and then indulged themselves. We anorexics arranged all the food very carefully, sighed and mooned over the look of it, felt wistful, then brought our own teas in on plates while the others ate. After the dancing there were games: Spin the Bottle naturally had pride of place. I got a peck off Joshua and glowed and giggled with pleasure.

I want to go home, I want to go home still played on inside my head like a mantra; but all in all, it was probably the nicest thing I've done for Valentine's Day ever. Where there's life there's hope.

PART FOUR:
TAMING

chapter one

'Who are all these people?' we asked each other. Something strange was happening at the unit. Stranger than usual, I mean. Staff were vanishing, replaced by an ever-changing cycle of agency aliens. Clive was gone. The dietician, Julie, was available less and less. I hadn't seen Fred and Fireman Sam for God knows how long. The air felt strange and confused.

Often nobody would turn up when Sally, Manda and I went to get our snacks:

'But we have to do it,' we'd remind each other, tremulously holding eyes, waiting, almost hoping one of us would give an out.

'We could have thrown them in the bin by now,' said Sally softly, 'and they wouldn't know it.'

The suggestion crackled in the air.

'Yes, I know, it's shit here,' Manda said at last. 'But we must have our snacks – to beat *him*. Come on.' Then she would start, and Sally would take her cue and start too, and I would follow suit. *Him* was another word for anorexia: the Voice, the Bastard, the Monkey.

'It's all falling to pieces,' people whispered. Time after time, nobody came to supervise our snacks. The Monkey howled louder. Nights were scary. Ruth had been doing night shifts; now she was gone, and my Scandinavian nurse no longer had the time to come and sit with me, busy with her duties. I could not sleep. I lay awake, and in the corridor outside I could hear Bethany crying.

'Why can't I have the new medicine?' she was sobbing.

A nurse was telling her, 'Because the doctor hasn't said so.'

'So what? What does he know about me? I never even see him.' Her pitch went up in desperation.

I squeezed my eyes up, feeling the hot tears well up behind the lids and seep out onto the pillow.

'Bethany, it must be his decision.'

'Why? Why do I have to wait to be given what I need by somebody who's practically a stranger?' She was shouting.

'Bethany, Bethany—'

'You could give them to me! Please!' The *please* was broken. My door was slightly ajar, and in the light from the corridor I saw the shadows of the speakers looming

216

large against my wall. They bobbed and stretched grotesquely.

'We haven't got the paperwork—'

'Paperwork!'

'We'll try to get him in the morning.'

'In the morning.'

'Yes.'

'That might not be any good.'

'Why not?'

'*Because I feel like killing myself tonight!*'

No, Beth, I pleaded with the shadows. *Please don't.*

Where were our nurses going? And our doctors? The other night a strange, big man I'd never seen before went prowling round the corridors at midnight and hovered in my doorway. I was petrified. Vague murmured answers circulated in the air. 'Overstretched and underfunded' was the common cry. Clive, they said, was ill. Manda had a different answer.

'They don't give two shits about us.' She said it distinctly and with perfect calm. 'What is this to them? A job. Making a living. Shift change, five o'clock, it's off home to their nice houses and forget all about this place. No, they don't care what becomes of us.' Three or four of us were taking refuge in the community room, curled up on chairs with our arms wrapped around our knees. We met each other's eyes uneasily. The place felt terribly empty. The air between us was tense. I was reminded dimly of those end-of-civilization films, where a chemical weapon or a superbug erases 99.9 per cent of the population, and the last survivors hide together in a room. I felt that if the planet's population were wiped out one afternoon, the inpatients of the unit would be the last to know it. The strange, uneasy days went crawling by, empty and neglectful. Each added a little more conviction to Manda's words, a mounting weight on our minds. Nerves frazzled.

On Mondays, in Community Meeting, we ordered our meals for the coming week. The hospital sent over box charts; we had to tick our options for each day. Sally and Manda and I could've filled out each other's. We always chose the same things. Plain fish, tomato pasta, vegetable hotpot.

It made things easier, knowing what was coming to you. But with the fading of the staff that all went haywire. It was a Tuesday at the end of February, getting close to lunch, and I was thinking, *Plain cod, potatoes, vegetables. I can deal with that.*

'Time to go!' said Chloe cheerfully, checking her watch and then looking sideways at Janet. There was a good ten minutes of lessons left, but Janet let us go anyway. Sally, Manda and I exchanged heavy looks and slowly followed the rest to the canteen. I got in the degrading queue; but as I shuffled closer to the counter, I saw something that caused me to freeze.

Two pieces of plain fish had been sent over. Not three. Two. The hospital had failed to send my meal. The shock was almost physical. Sally and Manda were ahead of me, and with worried, half-guilty glances backwards they snatched up the fish. I can't blame them. I would've done the same thing myself.

'I ordered plain fish,' I told the stranger serving, trying to restrain my panic.

She shrugged. 'It hasn't come.'

In horror I stared at the rest of the trays. Curry, swimming in fat. Battered cod with little pools of grease already grouping in the batter bubbles.

'I can't!' I stammered. 'I can't!'

'This is fish.' Unthinkingly the stranger plonked a battered side of cod in front of me. It took up *half the plate*. She added potatoes and vegetables.

Inside me the Monkey was screaming, '*You fat pig! You bitch!*' Grease seemed to radiate from the golden-brown monstrosity, the hunk of solidified fat. I must have been absorbing calories just breathing it. No one – *no one* had dared to try and make me eat such garbage in the past few months. *What the fuck gives them the right?* I was torn between screaming and crying, but I held myself in check. *I will not make a scene. I will dissect it. I will mess it about on the plate. I will not eat this SHIT. They cannot make me.*

Walking slowly, steadily, I headed for the table. There were few nurses about and most were strangers. But – *Oh no. No. Oh God, no* – who was sitting, waiting for me, trollish bulgy eyes honed in on me as I approached?

I raised an eyebrow at her, sat down and deliberately peeled the batter off the fish. To my surprise it came off in one single sheet, just like unwrapping a parcel. Underneath was an innocent white cod block just like Sally and Manda's.

'Jessica,' snapped the Troll, 'you have to eat the batter as well!'

'No I don't.'

'It's part of the main dish. Your meal plan says that you're to have a hospital main dish.'

'I ordered a fish square as a main dish. But there isn't one for me.'

'You have to eat the batter. It's part of the dish you've got.'

'*Tough.*' I appealed to another nurse; my pitch rose, and fear threatened to rob me of control. Luckily the other one sided with me. So in the end the batter was removed, and as I smirked, Eleanor Troll marched off glowering and bitching to record my misdemeanour in the book. But there was worse to come.

Over the next few days, more and more staff went away. Janet the teacher was ill. Meals grew steadily worse. For snacks we were all on our own now. We whispered fearfully behind their backs. The first crisis came when no main dish came over for me at all. I was forced under threat to swallow a plate of hotchpotch scrapings from the other trays: boiled rice, swede and baked beans. Misery, misery, one forkload at a time. Head down. Stomach heaving. *Eat it all.* But that was not the crunch. It came to the crunch when they placed the rice pudding in front of me. The dessert that I had ordered hadn't come, and as far as they were concerned this was just as good. Probably less fattening than chocolate cake and sauce. If it had been *anything* else, *anything* except rice pudding, it would've been OK. But I could not eat rice pudding. I can't now. I cried and I begged and I tried to explain; but nobody trusts a liar.

When I was about three years old, there was a television programme about a friendly wizard. I usually watched it sitting on the floor with my back against the sofa, my face by my nan's stockinged legs. I liked the wizard, and I liked his programme. There was only one thing that I didn't like. In the corner of the wizard's dungeon was a monster. It lived in a cauldron but it popped up sometimes. The monster and the liquid in the cauldron were the same: bubbly, grey, thick and horrid. Nan and Adam laughed at the monster but I hated it because it frightened me. It frightened me by giving me a sick feeling in my tummy and my throat. In the night I saw it in my head. Its bubbly grey skin made my flesh crawl and my mind squeal.

Later on, in primary school, I learned what it was made of. It was made of rice pudding.

The dinner ladies plopped the pudding onto my tray. I hated it. It looked like sick, and my own sick came into my throat. Then they made it worse. They took the jam and *plop*, dropped it in the middle. The other children stirred it round and round. The pudding went bright pink.

'Eat it all up,' they said, bearing down on me. Their aprons stretched up for ever.

'I can't, I can't.' My voice was high.

'You can't go out to play until you do.'

I sat there and the children went to play. The monster's skin was on my plate and it was bloody. I was going to be sick. Time crawled like snails on the rose bush in the garden. Misery misery. Let me go.

Then Mrs Walker came up to me. Her apron was white like an angel and the lights were bright behind her head.

'You don't have to eat it, lovely. You can go.'

I didn't cry, but I ran out of there and breathed against the wall. Nobody knew how bad it was to me, that pudding. Nobody knew that I was actually afraid. I didn't eat it in the infants and I didn't in the juniors. Nobody had asked me to eat it in high school. People knew I hated it and had a thing about it; it was a running joke among my friends. But they didn't know the night-terrors of early childhood that lumpy mass recalled.

All children are afraid of stupid things. Lions, vampires – why not rice-pudding monsters? We get older, and we lose the objects of the terror. But with an effort, often we can still recall the terror of the thing that lurked in the darkest corners at night, the thing that masked and yet personified our early notion that *this world is far from safe*. Facing the pudding at the unit brought that feeling back – the grey-white goo, the sick-sweet stench of it wafting up to my face. Unable to bear it any longer, I pushed the bowl away.

'Forget it,' I said savagely, tears dry now. '*You'd never understand.*'

chapter two

In that atmosphere of negligence, the Monkey's voice grew strong. Partly because I was weak, partly because food wasn't available, I started losing weight again. Weekend leave and visits were denied. I was devastated, begging Mum again to take me home for good:

'Sign me out, please sign me out.' On and on and on. 'I know you could do it, Mum. It's awful here. I don't know any of the nurses and I'm always scared. I'm trying to be good but they make me worse here. You could sign me out of here, couldn't you?'

'All right, I could,' she finally admitted. 'But, Jessica – I'm afraid.'

'Of what?'

'Of having no support.'

Guiltily I left it for the time.

The deterioration of the unit was due partly to absent staff, partly to lack of funds, partly to the jaded attitude of several senior staff members for whom we felt we were truly just specimens. Patient identity numbers on file. Naturally, there were other nurses who were genuinely caring. Pip was one, but for the most part these were younger trainee nurses without expertise in our problems.

I missed Clive. There were rumours that he wasn't coming back, that he was seriously ill, that he was dying. Julie had totally vanished.

Whatever bonds we patients started forming with our nurses broke down due to lack of communication. They did not know what we wanted or what we needed; they did not know us. All this came to a head one Monday morning at the Community Meeting.

In the community room was a whiteboard, and people used to scrawl messages on it with the markers: anything from '*Have a nice day*' to '*I fucking hate this prison.*' The previous day Robert had written: '*Reality: what happens between beers.*'

I thought that was pretty funny. I laughed and made some idle comment to the nurse on duty, then I forgot about it. I didn't know the nurse at all, and that was my fatal mistake.

Then came the Community Meeting. Robert had just five days to go before discharge. The mood was calm, and if not exactly cheerful, something approaching the soberly sane at the least. That was until the supervisor asked, 'Any complaints to make?'

This was routine for the end of a meeting. If someone had offended us we were meant to speak up. Hardly anyone did, except about disagreements over turns to use the phone. Not every patient got on with all the others at the unit, but there was certainly some kind of fellowship. Often we felt it was us against the staff or us against the world, and we did not squeal on each other. I think if someone had grassed on another patient, the others would have taken action. It was not done. Besides which, we hated Community Meetings, and basically wanted to end them as quickly as possible. There was a pause; nobody spoke. So the meeting would be closed, and it was going to be an OK day.

But the staff blew it.

The nurse whom I had spoken to put on a martyred voice: 'I have a complaint.'

Silence.

'Some people have been putting messages on the whiteboard,' she piped on piously, 'and some of us have been very upset by it.'

My stomach churned suddenly. Robert looked shocked and devastated – pending sane perhaps, but he was still fragile.

The quiet was hostile. We did not do this; we did not square off against each other. The sacred silent rule was being twisted; any minute it would break.

'Who would be upset by that?' asked Bethany coldly. 'That's just our joke.'

'I for one,' said the nurse. 'And also—'

OH GOD NO!

'Jess.' She pointed.

My heart stalled. The faces of my comrades turned to me, cold and closed. What was this betrayal?

'I did not say that!' I said hotly.

'Yes you did,' said the woman patiently. 'On the couch, you said—'

What the hell *had* I said? I did not even remember. Certainly, my meaning had been, *That's quite funny*, but somehow, being a stranger, this nurse had misinterpreted.

'You commented on it.'

'Because I liked it!'

'Well, some people find it quite offensive!' she sniffed.

'No they don't!' Now other voices chimed in.

'Oh yes, some do . . .' Then people were just shouting and protesting. The air had changed, and the suppressed friction screamed loud and proud. Robert looked close to angry tears. The calm was shattered.

Chloe, who hated tension of any kind, started crying quietly.

'All right, quiet, quiet.' The supervisor struggled to maintain order, but we were gone. All the frustrations and the bitterness at the neglect we'd suffered burst out suddenly. We were shouting at the staff and at each other. And all I'd meant was that I had liked Robert's joke.

Robert got up suddenly and said to the staff with a tearful exclamation, 'That's the trouble with you people! Whatever we do or say it's always wrong; it always condemns us and it's never good enough!'

He charged out. The truth of his words rang out clear. Rice pudding and the radiators – suddenly the air was full of similar accusations. Chloe cried harder; so did Sally. I did not cry. I was burning up. I hated them all, these stupid, stupid nurses, so qualified, graceful and patronizing – I wished they'd all leave and go martyr their heads off in Outer Mongolia or some-where. Because we sure as hell didn't need them!

I was never even sure if people blamed me for that episode, if they'd understood me or not in the tumult. Anyway, it was quickly forgotten: one mark of the fellow-ship was that we held no grudges, because we had all seen the worst of each other and had done just as wrong in our time. Nobody brought it up again overtly, and later Bethany was smiling, talking to me just as she always had. But at that meeting I had felt a new and terrible thing, a new fear. The pack must always have a victim for the rest to hold together, and in that moment I had known the terror of the one picked out for prey.

chapter three

'It *is* falling apart,' my mum agreed. 'I feel so sorry for these kids.'

'No one takes us anywhere any more,' I observed. 'The only time I ever get out for an hour is with you. No park trips, no village. There was meant to be a trip at half term to go bowling. But of course that was cancelled due to absent staff, or understaffing, or whatever else.'

'Sometimes I'm just tempted to take as many of you as I can in my car to the cinema or something.' My mother made a face.

'It would never be allowed.' *And you couldn't.*

Some of us had gone home over half term. I'd had just three days away. But on one of the days we had gone up to London, and visited my uncle with the pool. Everybody hugged and kissed me and said how glad they were to have me back. I ate according to my meal plan. I laughed and played computer games with my cousin. We sat out on the patio when the sun appeared briefly, and played a board game in the lounge. I wore a long, dark purple cardigan and didn't think I looked at all remarkable. Now I keep those photographs as grim reminders of my anorexic appearance. There are two. In one, my mother and I stand together in the kitchen with our arms around each other. My neck looks like a reed – you can see the structure of the cartilage – and my cheeks are sunken. My nose is red and looks too big for my face. My fingers look ready to snap. I am smiling, but my eyes are bright and desperate. In the second photo I am sitting on the couch, grinning and giving the camera the finger. Afterwards, my mother filled me in on the horrified looks and comments of my relatives behind my back. I just remember my uncle telling me, 'Drink a lot of milk!'

I'd hoped to stay at home for the entire holiday. But on Thursday we were obliged to go back for a weigh-in and, as I hadn't gained, I was not allowed back out. I wanted to kick and scream. I had tried to gain weight, really tried! Could it be because I moved around more outside the unit, or because it was easier to scrimp on portions without a nurse looking over my shoulder . . . ? The point was *I hadn't done it on purpose!* This was so unfair. But I went back without a fuss: I felt the heavy creeping resignation sliding over me like a blanket. Perhaps this was to be my life.

Now half term was over, and the kids came back. A large proportion of the staff did not. I still had no word of Clive – but someone had whispered *surgery*, and the word hung ominously in the quiet air.

Something was wrong with Manda. More wrong than usual, I mean. She was becoming isolated – Sally and Luke were an item now, and she was cut off somewhat from her best friend. Not that the new couple flaunted it; but the connection had been obvious from the start. We'd seen them dancing close on Valentine's Day; now they were holding hands, talking together in soft voices. The pair looked strange together, old and sad, she too thin and he emaciated.

'No good will come of that in the long run,' my mother predicted. 'They'll drag each other down. Or perhaps she'll long to be as thin as he is, to make sure she's still attractive to him.' I hoped she was wrong, but I thought she was probably right – in fact she was right already. Sally was sliding. Her weight dropped. Her mood dropped. When she went home at weekends her weight plummeted and she refused to come back. Sometimes her father had to carry her. Her beautiful hair turned brittle and came out in clumps when she brushed it. But she seemed to find some solace in Luke.

I wondered if competitiveness had added to his illness. The pressure to be light, to run fast. Be the fastest. Be the best. How ironic that this had been the outcome. I winced to think of him exercising, compelled on and on and looking like that. I was sad for the waste of such promise.

Meanwhile Manda went silent. That in itself was not unusual. She had phascs: sometimes she was loud and talkative in her distress, other times she was quiet. When she talked she told me stories: about a childhood, a good time like my own, when she and her sisters ran barefoot on beaches. She told me this when she was crouched against a radiator, crying, and I was crouched beside her. The sea rolled, the sun shone and the wind smelled of salt. There was no such thing as evil, there were no men and no terrible voices in her head. I went there with her in her memory. But now she had gone right into herself, and she didn't tell me stories any more.

She went about with a pale face, and dark shadows under her eyes. Her black hair was brittle and her eyes took on a staring and distracted quality. Yet she ate the same as ever. In unit school she was silent.

When the scanty staff discovered it, she'd been at the

business for about four days. Manda had turned bulimic. Not an uncommon thing with anorexics. When they are hospitalized and forced to eat they sometimes do it. Silent protestation. The Voice, or Monkey, grasping horribly to life. And being Manda, she did it with a determination and totality that horrified me – all except the Monkey. That bugger thought it was brilliant. Every time she ate – or drank – Manda would simply leave the table afterwards, quietly go into a toilet cubicle and vomit. Of course, nobody watched her or supervised. Far too overstretched and understaffed. Her words rang in my head again: *They don't give two shits about us . . . it's just a job.* I found her clinging to the radiator again, having been found out, silent tears streaming down her face. What could I do? I crouched beside her, looked into her face with shock in a *Do you want to tell me?* gesture. She met my gaze with wild eyes.

'If I even had a cup of coffee,' she whispered hoarsely, 'even a black one, I would have to throw it up.'

'But there's no calories in coffee,' I said, aghast.

'I know.'

'But is it – isn't it hard?'

'With fingers, yes. But there are ways. Toothbrushes. Forks.'

I gagged.

234

The place was thrown into confusion. This always happened when somebody went right down. Now, with the absence of staff, it was just total chaos.

I'm getting out of here, I thought forcefully. *I like these people. They are good. But I can't go down like this. Can't take this path. This is a sinking ship. I'm different – I'm not as sick as them.* And suddenly, the need for that was stronger even than the Monkey. Something clicked inside my head. I must leave. Whatever it took, I must leave. Everything else could wait: thinness, control, perfection must be shelved. *I must get out of here.*

Light. Something had been lifted from my vision, or perhaps I had clawed my way out from under it at last. Things added up – *eat = get out* – that had made no sense before. So I began to eat faster, clearing my plate before the other girls, back to normal speed. Once I started, broke the painstaking rituals of anorexic dining, it was easier. Food goes in the mouth. Automaton. I chewed, swallowed, barely tasting; I felt nothing for the food, it was simply a means to escape. I lifted my plate and took it to the sink while the nurses stared in bewilderment. I began to beg my mother with new vigour:

'Look at this place!' I appealed. 'How can I get better here? Take me home. Of course I'll eat. I'll even put weight on. Mum, I've seen the other option to it now – and it's so much worse!'

She said nothing for long while, but looked at me thoughtfully. We were in the little visiting room again. The Scrabble was on the table but we hadn't opened it. This was the beginning of March, a new month, and I had been a patient since 27 December. In two days' time I had a major review scheduled: consultants, teachers, nurses, dietician were all supposed to be there.

'OK, here's what I think,' said my mother finally. 'You don't need to be here all the time. I don't want you to be here. But I don't want to be on my own with this—'

'Care in the Community!' I blurted. This was the official name for what they offered at the clinic I'd attended back in December, when I saw Sarah, the Irish child psychiatrist. I didn't know what else it might entail and I didn't care. Anything – anything would be better than this place. And it would mean living at home.

'I think we should find out about that,' Mum agreed. 'But in the meantime I still want you to be here sometimes.'

'I want to go to school.'

'That has to be positive.'

'I want to have days, at least, when I don't have to

come here at all. When I can forget this hell-hole even exists.'

So we got down a big piece of paper from one of the pads, and I found my timetable from school. We got a thick black marker pen, and between us, we drew up our grand dream plan for my complete recovery. It included mornings and afternoons in school, some therapy sessions in the unit and visits to Sarah. I would sleep at home. When we were done it looked so good and right and positive. We hugged.

'This is going to work,' I said, and I believed it. 'I will get better, Mum. I want to.'

We awaited the review.

chapter four

I feared, as soon as I entered the shaded office, that things would not be going our way at all that afternoon. The blinds were drawn, and the professionals sat round on chairs with faces closed. In that poor light, the white-board gleamed with savage readiness to boast my latest crimes. My friend-nurse Clive was still missing.

I stopped dead.

In Clive's chair sat the Troll.

What the hell—? What right did she have to be here? It was an outrage. She smiled slowly, met my eyes across the room. I knew she was thinking of batter.

'I've taken on the duty of a personal nurse to you, Jessica,' she told me. My teeth ground at her voice. 'Unit regulations state you must have two personal nurses at all times.'

Ohhhhfuckfuckfuckfuckfuck!

Julie, the pleasant dietician, was also missing. Jane Wright sat glowering, hard as steel in her place of power

238

at the front. Fred and Fireman Sam cowered together in a corner, glancing nervously from side to side.

The meeting began with a tone of reserved positiveness: maybe I was doing a little better. Eating more anyway. Maybe even being more co-operative. Then it was our turn. Mum and I glanced at each other; sitting side by side, we faced the wall-like army of diplomas, MScs and PhDs. I could look in their faces again. Seizing the tentative hope, we put forward our case; held our thick-marker timetable between us. In a calm voice I explained our plan.

A weighted pause.

'Well, I must say we're surprised,' said Jane Wright at last. What? Had no one dared to challenge her authority in the history of the unit? 'We all still think that Jessica needs to be here.'

How the fuck would you know? I almost exploded. *You haven't even seen me in a month!*

'You can't pick and choose what the unit can offer you,' said Eleanor, shaking her head over our chart. Janet had a tiny smile on her face that she was trying her best to hide. But her eyes twinkled behind her glasses. I saw she was touched and impressed.

'But I thought,' my mum protested, 'that you treated people here as individuals.'

'Oh we do,' said Eleanor, smirking widely. 'Of course.'

Yeah, I thought, *you give out different-size puddings according to how tall we are. Oh, the liberty of it.*

'But we must have some rules and regulations. You can't just take what you want.'

More silence.

'What about Care in the Community?' my mum asked suddenly. 'I thought we might look into that.'

'Mrs Hassan, there *is* no Care in the Community,' replied Wright, and to this day, I have never been able to regard that as anything but an outright lie. I cannot understand why she said it. What was her motivation? Because there *was* Care in the Community, as we found out later, and Jane Wright was in contact with it. Not brilliant care, granted. But to say it didn't exist?

Back then we didn't really know the system, and that is why what my mum did next is so incredibly brave. She is proud like I am, and she's clever, and she loathed the humiliation of that review. More importantly she believed in me.

'In that case . . .' she said.

Do it, do it, do it! I urged silently. *I swear I will behave.*

'I am going to sign Jessica out today.'

And having said it, she did. With the signing of that paper on that day the wheels were set swiftly in motion.

I have never known a bureaucratic system move so fast. I suppose, at bottom, they just wanted the bed back. And afterwards, Fred came up to my mother and told her that he was notifying Sarah's clinic; that yes, there would be assistance for her within the community, and that if things went badly wrong again they'd not refuse to treat me. Basically the opposite of everything Jane Wright and the Troll had just said. Bizarre and confusing; but who cared about that now? I was going! I was out of there!

It took effect that day. I sang as I packed up my few possessions in my little room. The Monkey was quiet, cowed by the bounty I had earned in disobeying it, and it all looked like plain sailing from then on.

Suddenly Chloe walked in. 'Oh – you're going home.' She meant for overnight leave; it was Friday. Something inside me deflated.

'Y-yes,' I said.

'Till when?'

'Till – for good.'

Her mouth dropped open. I reiterated: 'I'm leaving.'

'For ever?'

I nodded dumbly. 'Well – I'm coming back on Monday to say goodbye.' It was Eleanor's idea that I return. A petty parting shot, perhaps. When people were discharged, they were usually given a gift in Community Meeting. It made things less abrupt and sudden for the others, and they wanted to disguise the real nature of my leaving. What were they afraid of? Revolution? Possible. Sometimes it seemed pending.

Chloe stared at me for a long moment. Was she angry? No. At last she choked out: 'I don't know whether to laugh or cry!' And we flung ourselves into an embrace.

The news ripped through the unit like a bushfire. But I left quickly that night; it hadn't sunk in, even in my own brain, that this was actually real. To be honest, perhaps I was cowardly. I didn't want to face them. But on Monday I returned, sat through a final Community Meeting; the staff airbrushed the thing to make it sound as though I'd been discharged, but the others knew the truth. The present was a mug wrapped in birthday paper. Everyone's always was. I unwrapped it publicly and thanked them in the way you thank people for mugs. Then came the real goodbyes. The hugs and the well-wishing. The votes of confidence. The sentiments beneath were very mixed: genuine pleasure, envy, anger, real hope for my future perhaps. Sally hugged me tightly; so did Manda, but there was something cool and almost angry in her small face when we drew apart. I could not blame her. She sent me a message from her aged eyes.

I was right, wasn't I? That first day we met. You were never like me. You have not seen what I have seen, endured what I've endured. You still have a chance of a good life. That was stolen from me long ago. I know that I should want you to be happy, and in most of my being I do. But I envy you, Jessica Hassan. You have what I deserved.

Then out to the car, a flurry of movement. I sat in the front seat, the engine revved – and as we pulled away for the final time I threw my hands into the air and screamed for pure joy.

'Never, never!' I shouted like a manic Peter Pan. 'I am never going back there!'

'Never,' Mum agreed.

chapter five

Those first days back at home were easy. The Monkey had been proven indisputably wrong by the nightmare of the past months, and I was willing to do anything – anything – to avoid its twisted clutches. I would say anything, do anything, smile like a madman. If someone had served me up a slab of chocolate gateau I might well have eaten it. The very first morning at home – home for good – was a Tuesday, and my mother brought my breakfast to me on a tray: two Weetabix and a small banana. I weighed seven stone two, and at that precise moment I honestly didn't care. I ate it easily and happily and then I went to school.

Compared to what I'd seen it was heaven. I could not believe how easy everything was. Last time I'd been in school, I'd usually been hiding a calculator under the desk, totting up imaginary calories over and over. When I couldn't get away with that I did it in my head. Now that my mind was not filled up with raging buzzing bees

I actually listened to the lessons, in an idle sort of way. It was all child's play! Even maths, which I've never liked, and consequently always been bad at. Now suddenly I could do sums. Before, school timetables had seemed restrictive – now I knew what it was to be *utterly free* from half past three every day. People were being *nice* to me, and I enjoyed myself. Predictably, I was something of an icon to the other pupils: *Behold, the girl who went nuts!* At first I loved it. The girls now shot envious looks at my thinness, the boys smouldered with a quiet respect for the extremes I'd gone to in defiance of authority. Because they were getting older, I suppose, a little of what I'd felt was starting to catch up with them. The only comment I heard murmured once behind my back was: 'She's skinnier than Katie Albright.'

I walked home happily at a normal pace, singing aloud for sheer freedom.

The second day home I got up: 'Am I going to school again?'

'I don't think so,' said Mum. 'I mean, you went yesterday – we don't want to rush things.'

'But I want to! I liked it!'

'Oh!' Surprise. 'Well, all right then! Good!'

I genuinely wanted to be normal. To be as absolutely distanced from the awful unit as I possibly could. But the past months didn't just vanish. There were barriers now: I knew I was distanced from the others. They knew nothing, they were still all children, and I knew . . . way too much. But for that time I just chose to ignore it, and pretended everything was fine – no, everything was *wonderful*, I loved everyone and everything, I was just delighted to be back. I laughed at disrupted lessons, enjoyed them. For after all, what did work matter? Freedom was the important thing, to live and breathe free air.

One day in form class, not long after my return, a boy I barely knew came up to me suddenly and laid his wrist across the table. I looked down. Across his veins he'd drawn some superficial scratches with a compass or nail scissors, breaking several layers of skin.

'I tried,' he told me darkly. 'See, I did try.'

'Don't.'

'Are you on happy pills?'

I paused. 'I take anti-depressants.'

'Will you bring some in for me, Jessica? Please? I need them. Really.'

Here was a new piece to the puzzle. Maybe not all of the ordinary kids were so ordinary after all.

'I don't think I ought to do that,' I said uneasily. 'They don't seem to do much anyway. Is there maybe someone you could talk to?'

'No. There's nobody. Nobody understands. I cut myself a lot, you know.'

'Oh. Don't.'

The rumour of the happy pills spread fast, and I was even more of a celebrity. Some of them had heard of Seroxat, including the risks involved. I was the next most interesting thing to a drug addict. Weird fame brought uneasy pleasure.

On Tuesdays I went to the GP's practice to be weighed. A cheerful Scottish nurse supervised the new weigh-ins, for which I had to strip down to a T-shirt, socks and tights. I always wore tights even under trousers, because I was always cold. I still do in the winter. They measured me as five foot three, which I already knew. These were not fancy 0.1-of-a-kilo scales like the unit's. They had a shaky dial similar to our bathroom's. I hated getting onto them that first time. I was tempted to shut my eyes. But I couldn't resist a quick peek. The nurse looked at the dial – I winced – what was she going to say?

'Seven stone two. Well, that's not too bad!' she exclaimed brightly. 'Thank you, dear.'

'You mean' – I almost gasped for joy – 'I don't have to put weight on?'

'Well, you could do with some more. But there, you've got plenty of time.'

I looked at Mum, unable to believe my ears – in the unit, the pressure to gain weight was like an anvil grinding down on you.

'I'm worried that she doesn't get her period,' my mum said.

'Oh that' – the nurse waved her hand dismissively – 'I wouldn't worry. What are you – fourteen? Heaps of time. If you don't have it at eighteen then I'd worry.'

'But she used to have it; she started at eleven.'

'Ah well' – the nurse smiled – 'they can often be irregular the first few years.'

Still, I had promised my mum I would gain weight, and I didn't dare refuse a bite of anything she gave me. Next week my weight was the same, so I ate more, and it continued to creep up, a little at a time. I hated bulk – it still seemed heavy in my little stomach – so dried fruits, nuts and calorie-dense cereal bars proved useful. They also didn't feel too much like junk food, so they went down easily. More easily than, say, a packet of crisps. Now up a pound, now down half, rarely more drastic than that. I kept smiling. I mostly avoided mirrors, but I could feel myself growing bigger.

I had not been home long when I had an appointment

to see Sarah James at her clinic again. I cringed to think what I'd been like the last time she had seen me. Six months ago, huddled up in my black coat, crying, snivelling and starving but denying it with venom.

The clinic was the same as I remembered it, and so was Sarah's room. Sarah, however, was not the same. She was pregnant. I blinked and started when I saw that. Then I smiled and congratulated her. She thanked me, grinning genuinely.

I strode into my first session with her, head up, smiling, eyes ahead. I looked happy and I felt it. The freeness of everything still delighted me, the simple knowledge that I could go home at the end of the school day, could dress and brush my teeth and do my homework at whatever time pleased me best; didn't have to book and queue for a shower. Feeling safe at night, warm in my own bed. The lack of screams and wails. It was spring, and every leaf seemed greener, brighter than I'd ever known them, and so intricately patterned. Things I had never noticed in my life before were piercingly beautiful. Sunlight bright on water. The whorls on a tree bole astonished me. A small bird taking flight filled me with sudden awe. The way a flower blooms and dies and blooms again was hope and promise.

Sarah and I talked of all sorts of things. School. Family. The baby she was expecting. I smiled and I laughed, and I went off on tangents, and I commented on little things about the office and the pictures on the walls.

'Well, Jessica, I'm amazed,' said Sarah at last, putting down her pen and smiling. 'You are not the girl I met six months ago.'

'This is the real me,' I told her eagerly. 'Without the illness.'

'But you know you're still too thin.'

Crunch. A bucket of ice-cold water came crashing over my head. I said my weight was creeping up before, but it really wasn't significant; I was effectually staying just the same and I was happy. I looked OK, I thought. But I couldn't be bigger than this. I made some evasive comment and kept smiling.

'Well, I'll still want to see you once a week,' Sarah said. 'And once a month you will have an appointment with the consultant psychiatrist. But that really is all we have time for today.' She looked at the clock. 'How is next Wednesday for you?'

I skipped out of the office. Worry about tomorrow when it came. I was alive and I was free again, and now I knew how much that mattered!

chapter six

'*Hey, fat arse!*'

I froze. I was leaving the school building at the end of March, coming out of a covered walkway. I heard the random comment shouted from a door. Of course, of course it was aimed at me! *I* was a fat arse! I knew it! I was wearing a black coat – it was still cold; my hands went to my backside in a vain attempt to gauge its hugeness. I gulped. Then I ran home in a panic and related the tragedy to my mother. Patiently she went through the reasoning. Random insults. Childishness. I was underweight.

Things were getting harder again. I was under pressure to gain at least another few pounds, mostly from my mother and the clinic's consultant psychiatrist. The psychiatrist's name was Dr Richards. A large part of her job was spent in counselling teenage anorexics. She seemed to know a lot about the illness, and she seemed like a pretty nice lady. She was clever. She was calm. She was coherent. And she was absolutely enormous.

251

'*You gonna listen to HER?*' screeched the Monkey when I saw her first. The answer, from all of me: '*Noooo way.*' I called her Dr Fatty in my mind. Maybe for somebody with schizophrenia or OCD she would've been a lifeline. But the anorexic needs to trust that her carers know what they are doing when it comes to food. Sarah was slim and looked healthy.

The voice of the Monkey waxed loud and strong. The label on my trousers said size eight but in the bathroom mirror I was big.

I began to exercise in secret. Sit-ups. Then they took a hold of me again and I repeated and repeated them. Worry gnawed hard at my brain. I snuck off to do them in the middle of the day. Eventually, inevitably, my mum caught me at it: screaming row. In my next session with Sarah she banned me.

'Why not?' I whined. 'Exercise is good.'

'But a certain kind of exercise is very bad for you. You have what we call an obsessive personality, Jessica. And combining anorexia with OCD – well, it's a recipe for disaster. Obsessive compulsive behaviour can ruin people's lives.'

I looked at her.

'Once I treated a boy,' said Sarah, 'who could not get out of his house in the morning. The reason was the buttons on his shirt. He had certain requirements for doing them up, and as OCD took hold they became bigger and more elaborate. Until in the end he could not leave his house to get to school on time.'

Just like my sit-ups, I thought. The story scared me and I vowed to stop them.

I had huge mood swings. As I sprawled on the floor in the front room, blasting heavy rock through my head-phones, Adam came in and turned the television on.

'Turn it. The fuck. Off,' I said warningly.

'You can listen to that anywhere. This is the only room I can watch TV in.' He sat down on the couch.

'*I was here first!*' I screamed, getting up and flinging my headphones at him – they bounced harmlessly off his leg and settled on the carpet.

'*Turn this shit off!*' I dashed to the TV and hammered the off switch – Adam turned it back on again, using the remote. Then he picked up my headphones and CD player, hoisted me over his shoulder and calmly deposited me in the hall, where I lay on the carpet and screamed.

Other times I went manic with laughter. The cat chasing its tail made me cackle till I cried. I locked myself away alone and wrote my diary a lot, damning everyone and claiming that they didn't understand. I felt fat, disgusting and disgusted. I screamed at my mother – after everything she'd done for me – and she screamed back although I was so scared and miserable.

'But you're thin!' she'd cry as I poked miserably at a plate of food – theoretically I was still keeping to the unit meal plan, but scrimping and cutting around the edges again.

'I feel fat,' I snivelled.

'Oh my God! You are so, so selfish, Jessica! You are *so* self-absorbed! How can feeling fat matter more to you than what you're doing to this family? I still have your grandmother to think about, you know! Just because she's in a home doesn't mean I can just abandon her!'

'You don't understand! Oh my God, you have no idea what it's like in my head!'

'In *my* head. *Me, me, me.* You are self-obsessed, Jessica. Why don't you stop thinking about yourself for a change?'

Afterwards we'd both feel terrible but the damage was done. The fractured state of that relationship caused deep grief.

Rachel and Joanne called, but I found excuses not to go out with them. I didn't want anyone to see me like this: fat, weak and disgusting. And a self-obsessed bitch now, to boot. Besides, they would expect me to smile and laugh with them.

'So you're better now?' Rachel asked hopefully over the phone.

Jesus Christ, I almost snapped at her. *Yeah, better, Rachel. Let's go out for burgers.* But I only spoke like that to my mother and my brother, who I knew would take it from me; to Rachel I said, 'Better than I was.'

'So you want to come ice-skating Saturday?'

'Er, I can't.'

'How come?'

'We . . . have visitors.' Crap lie.

'Oh. Well, how about going shopping on Sunday?'

'You and Joanne go shopping,' I told her forcefully. 'Maybe next time.'

Later, when the phone rang, I refused to answer it. I could just see myself bursting into tears in the middle of town, or wanting to walk super-fast; and what would I do when they wanted to go to Pizza Hut for lunch? *Oh my God oh my God oh my God.* I placed my head in my hands and sat against the radiator – so cold. *I do not want to go shopping, Rachel. I do not want to look at pretty clothes. I do not want to see myself in mirrors . . . oh please, won't you just go without me? Just get on with your lives. I'm not good enough for you, I'm a loser. I'll use you just like I've used everybody else. Please just forget about me, I'll only drag you down . . .*

One day I was struggling within myself and keeping

quiet about it; unfortunately, my mum had run out of low-fat meats and fish for dinner. She put sausages in front of me. Fireworks is an understatement. My poor brother looked from one to the other of us – even the cat was hissing. I ate the sausages at last, tears choking me, with the threat of the unit hanging over my head. But the culmination was me running off to lock myself in my room without dessert. I screamed into the pillow and wept. Then eventually I sat and listened to the Monkey's awful voice, gnawing and hissing in my brain.

'*No one can save you.*'

'*Fuck you. I can save myself.*'

'*How?*'

'*By just carrying on. By eating my supper, by not exercising more than I'm allowed and so on.*'

'*You're fat.*'

'*Fuck off, I'm not fat.*'

'*They shout at you and call you horrible things.*'

'*I will save myself. Please, God, if you're there.*'

'*Move, you lazy bitch!*' (I was huddled against my bed.) '*Burn calories!*'

'*I'm not meant to exercise in the house.*'

'*What about those sausages?*'

'*Well, I didn't have dessert.*'

'*SO? THEY'RE STILL FULL OF FAT! OH GOD, YOU*

256

*ATE THEM, YOU SICK BITCH! YOU MAKE ME WANT
TO PUKE! HOW COULD YOU?'*

'*I don't KNOW! STOP CONFUSING ME!'*

'*You need to be punished. You need to diet to make up for
your sins.'*

And so on. Then I wanted to go apologize and make
it up with my mum, but she had shut herself in her
bedroom. The blank, closed look of the cream door
made an impassable barrier, shouting *Barred* into my
face. At last I crossed the hallway to my brother's room
and knocked. We'd been arguing savagely lately, but
the desperation in my face or voice must have over-
ridden that. Things might be screwed up, thanks to me,
but he was still my brother. Adam ushered me into his
room and we sat down on the floor.

'Listen, Jess,' he said, shaking his head. 'You've got
to stop this. I think Mum's going to go nuts or something and then what will we do?'

'I can't,' I wailed. 'You can't just stop. All the psychiatrists and everyone say it's a long, painful process . . .'

'I don't give a shit what the psychiatrists say! What
do they know about it? Look, you've got a choice: stop
now, or Mum goes nuts. Simple.'

'But – but how do I stop it?' Suddenly I was listening.
Adam was speaking to me forcefully and with feeling.

He sounded like he knew what he was doing. And I sure as hell didn't know. Was salvation here at last, this simple, and being offered by my *brother* of all people?

'You have to eat,' Adam said, and shrugged.

'I do eat.'

He snorted. 'Barely.'

'I eat what it says on my meal plan—'

'Jess, don't lie. I've seen the sort of thing you do with food – crumble and break it up, mush it around and sneak bits into the bin. Cry until you get away with less than you should.'

'Well – well, what should I eat?'

'Anything. Have some toast.'

'I can't! I can't!'

He was getting frustrated. 'What is wrong with you? If you don't, you're just choosing anorexia. You're saying, *I love anorexia more than anything else!*'

So I did it. We went downstairs together and we made some toast, and I ate the toast, with butter on, even after the lard-ridden sausages. I did it like an automaton. Then I dashed upstairs in desperate hope and hammered on my mum's door:

'Mum! *Mum!* I ate toast!'

No reply. I went back to my room and cried myself to sleep.

chapter seven

My fourteenth birthday came and went. I barely noticed it happen. Fourteen! I felt about eighty-five most days. Could I really be just fourteen years old? I was so bloody tired.

I had changed so much in the last year. I had never sworn as a child: *fuck* wasn't even a word in our house. *Ffff—* was a threat. Now I said fuck all the time, and I wrote it, and my mother didn't seem to care at all. The world was permeated with unending ugliness: why not use coarse words to describe it? I was torn up inside. Only the threat of the unit was keeping me eating.

Often I walked down the street with tears in my eyes. Everywhere was hate, pain, ugliness. I remembered the tales from the unit. I looked at houses with the curtains drawn and orange lights behind them in the evening and I wondered what atrocities that glow masked. My so-called friends were aliens. I had seen whole worlds they couldn't dream existed. I knew the horrors of life.

I couldn't eat, sometimes, not because of fear of fat, but because sickness and sadness at the world were choking me, filling me up, and there was no room left for food.

Nonetheless, there was some triumph in the fact I was fourteen. I had lived to a new age. Survived. There were times I had assumed I would be dead by now, and I wasn't. Life was grey, and I wavered from self-pity to self-loathing to a blazing and obscenity-filled anger. I did sit-ups, but stopped when Mum caught me doing them. She didn't speak to me for three days.

Then I had an idea.

'Mum,' I said, 'if I was just allowed to exercise in a general way – say swimming – the minimum amount for health, I wouldn't have to worry so much. Twenty minutes, three times a week.'

'Well, I suppose we could try it,' she said after thought. 'But only on the condition that you don't do any sit-ups or anything else. The swimming would be everything.'

'Deal,' I said happily. How simple. No more worries. I should've thought of that sooner. And for a little while it worked.

The first time I returned to swimming, I got in and did twenty minutes of lengths – no messes, no fuss, no problem. That week I lost weight, so we made a deal: if I was going to swim I ate a little piece of chocolate first to give me the energy I needed. I gulped it down, despising it, feeling it clog and choke my throat with filth. But it was worth it. Swimming became my exorcism. If I swam well I could eat with less guilt. Afterwards I felt nice and relaxed. My hair was soft and curly.

At the end of May my mother broke her arm. In a rush, she tripped and fell down the steps outside our front door. The rest of that day was a flurry of activity. My mum returned from casualty with her arm in plaster. It needed to be in a cast for some weeks. That meant major changes.

'You're going to have to take more responsibility – both of you,' she told us. 'I'm expecting you to be grown up about this . . .' she added, looking directly at me. She kept on at me to try harder, not to be so sad, to be of more practical help around the house.

And I was. I did the dishes, hoovered, hung the washing up. The way I saw it, I was doing everything that could be asked of me – even making my own breakfast and lunch. But my mum was tired out and I was still troublesome. Mental illness is a selfish thing. Our mantra to each other was, '*You don't appreciate how hard I work!*'

We had a joint session with Sarah, in which she asked us both to keep a 'feel-good diary'. Well, actually *ordered*. She gave me the book – a bunch of coloured paper of the type they use in primary school. On the front was written:

Jessica's
Feel-good
Diary

in Sarah's disjointed letters. Underneath the words were placed five stickers: shiny teddy bears in different colours, and each one '= a percentage'. I was supposed to rate each day by sticking on a teddy bear. I nearly laughed at that. Shit, couldn't I just write the numbers on? These were just the sort of stickers that you get in primary school for good work or for good behaviour or being the day's best tidier. But I controlled myself, for the sake of Sarah's feelings. A blue teddy was for 100 per cent; the green was the lowest – 60. There aren't any lower than that. Apparently no day can be less than 60 per cent good. I saw the oversight at once, and she knew I saw it; I glanced at her and my lips twitched. 'Play along,' she asked me with her eyes. There were lines around them, though they were not old, and I knew that she, like me, had seen a lot of days lower than 60.

After every entry my mum was supposed to write her comments: to say when she was disappointed but also note and appreciate when I'd done well. It is a strange book – fluctuating from bright, dry and articulate to angry and selfish and mad.

FRIDAY
Jessica:
Ok. I talked to Sarah today (hi), and when I did my lunch I had to use a different kind of bread than usual. Started a story and thought it rather good but it's private right now as it's in very rough stages. Went swimming. Felt quite nice after cos I get satisfaction from the exercise and my hair's all nice and curly now. Went on the Internet and chatted to my Internet friends. Practised piano. I tried a different dessert that I've never had but I don't want to have it again cos it wasn't very nice. I want to carry on my story.

Mum:

Jessica prepared and ate her own break-fast and lunch as required by her eating plan. Well done, Jess! She hung out the washing and did the washing-up as I have one arm in plaster. Thanks for your help, Jess, I appreciate it.

They were mixed days. I think my real self was in control a good portion of the time now, not the Monkey. I sort of wince at what my mum wrote; trying so hard to show me I was valued – because, you see, she doesn't talk like that. Oh, of course she says thank you and stuff, but by nature she's not overly emotional. As a small child, when I wanted cuddles (which was always) I had to go up and clamber on her, and my dad was far more at ease with all that. After my dad died she changed, tried to be more openly affectionate:

'Do you love me?'

'Millions and millions.'

But it's not really her, and these diary entries don't sound like her voice. The above day had a yellow teddy – 70 per cent. It's the first entry and I think I made an effort to play Sarah's game. Sunday is more satirical:

> Today I wrote a poem called 'How Westlife Died'. Ha ha ha ha ha ha etc. PS found a pen. Went to the shop, played on the dance mat, went on the Internet . . . got bored. Went for a walk, typed up Part 4 of a story I'm posting on the Internet, but I did three paragraphs, went to unplug something and unplugged the computer, work unsaved.

I've given the day a blue bear, 100 per cent, and written after it '*for the poem*'. Underneath I've drawn a skull and crossbones and written '*for erasing my own writing*'.

My mother's comments pick up the arch mood:

> Jessica was feeling a bit restless on and off today and found walking lifted her spirits. This included a trip to the shop for me, which was very helpful — thanks, Jess. I was pleased, Jess, that you were able to have a different dessert today. Well done!

What she did not know was that I was doing sit-ups once again behind her back, and the next day she caught me at it. The diary entry looks like an explosion – our scrawling scripts crawling all over each other. She wasn't going to write in it at first, I remember:

'I have nothing good to say!'

'Well, you have to write something.' I shrugged. 'Sarah said so.' I act like a real bitch sometimes, but I tend to win battles of words. The final statement on the page is mine:

And in response to the comment from my mum: 'All you did tonight was what you wanted to' – oh yeah. Studying for assessment tests. Par-tay.

chapter eight

Anorexia can go hand in hand with OCD: obsessive compulsive disorder. I was manifesting OCD literally years before That Diet kicked in; and it's all tied up with guilt. When I was ten I went through a 'confession' phase, which lasted for maybe a year, when I was convinced that *everything I did* would somehow have bad consequences for other people. It usually had to do with hygiene. If I told my mum about it, and she said it was OK, then it would be OK. And I do mean everything I did. A confession would be something like:

'I . . . I . . . I think I touched my nose . . . and there might have been snot on my finger – and then, you know, when I washed my hands it might've gone onto the soap. And then I got a plate out of the rack!'

And worse. The damn things went on for ever.

I had a similar thing with electric plugs: someone told me once that leaving plugs in overnight is a fire hazard. I had a lamp by the side of my bed; each night

I'd unplug it before I put the light out. Then I'd get up again and check it, feeling about in the dark. Then I'd wonder: did I really check the plug, or just imagine that I'd checked it? Up again, ad infinitum. People can get OCD much worse than that – to the point they can't leave their houses. Bound up in chains of iron with their fears and obsessions.

Fear is another major factor. Since ancient times, people have used ritual and repetition as a safeguard against terror, as a search for certainty in a chaotic-seeming world. I was scared of everything when I was small.

Anorexia provided ample material for obsessive rituals. First, it had been the spot exercises. Now, swimming was to be my exercise, and for the Monkey to be satisfied that I had swum adequately, certain requirements had to be met.

Firstly, I had to swim lengths for exactly half an hour, then add on two more as I could not believe the evidence of the clock. I could not stop, talk to anyone or bump into anyone, adjust my goggles or do anything else but swim. My hair had to be tightly arranged in two plaits, then tied into one, in case stray hairs got in the way and spoiled the effects of the exercise. My fingernails and toenails should be not too long or short. I had to go to the toilet before I exercised, or it would all be invalid. To help me remember that I'd really been, rather than just imagining it, I used to fasten a piece of wool around my wrist. In the toilet cubicle I'd take it off and put it on the bin, and check it when I got out to see I had been there. Goggles had to be adjusted in the mirror to see they were the right way up, and swimsuit straps had to be straight.

And of course, I couldn't trust the evidence of my own eyes regarding any of this – so my poor mother had to check for me by sitting in the café and watching. Afterwards I put her through the third degree: was that half an hour? Was it really? Yes, but where was the second hand on the clock? Maybe the final minutes wouldn't count? Was the wool on my wrist? Was it gone when I got in the pool? Was it really gone? Wait – did I really ask if that was half an hour or I had I just imagined it? And so on.

This didn't happen all at once. It built up over time. It's a pretty typical example of the structures that obsessions create. And if one thing – one tiny thing among that great web of requirements – went wrong, the whole session was void. In which case – well, I'd be enormous, the planet would collapse, mighty mountains would be riven asunder and the horsemen of the apocalypse would descend in fiery wrath to fetch my soul to burning hell. I would ask my mother again and again about it afterwards – on and on and on. After she broke her arm, my mother had to take me on the bus:

'Leisure centre, please.'

The driver looked ironically at the cast on her arm and asked, 'Going back for another bout?'

She still took me. Afterwards I questioned and I questioned. My mum put a lock on her door but I cried outside. We screamed. We both cried. Once, after catching me still locked in the cycle of sit-ups (to make up for bad swimming), I thought she was on the verge of suicide.

'What is my life?' she asked, and locked herself in the bathroom, away from me. She told me to just go away, she didn't want to see me any more.

Utter terror gripped me: the medicine cabinet was in there. She could not do this! We had already lost our father. Adam and I would be orphaned. I would have to kill myself as well. That would be the only solution. And as I was undoubtedly going to hell now anyway, that wasn't much consolation. I sat and wailed on the landing, rocking with my arms around my knees, feeling like my heart was being ripped to pieces inside me.

But the fever-pitch moment passed, and she did not

harm herself. There was probably no reason to believe she would – it was just my confusion and terror making me think she might. She was stronger than me, perhaps, or just not inclined to self-destruction. But she would not show me her face, she locked herself away from me, so I went and hid by my bed, shaking with sobs of repentance.

Prayer. Last refuge of the desperate. I used to write my prayers on paper. They're mostly pretty stupid. I often tried to bribe God. I had never stopped believing in a God, and a pretty much omnipotent God at that. But I questioned the benevolence of a being who could make such a dark world as this. Such a terrible being as me. Such a fiend as the Monkey. Such relentless, needless evil as the patients at the unit had endured. What kinds of gifts were these?

So in those days I would kneel by my bed and plead and threaten, bargain with a cool and distant power. It rarely worked. I had a sense of being crushed down, not being lifted up, which cannot have come from any god worth worshipping, but rather from a bad place inside me, where there is wailing and gnashing of teeth for certain.

chapter nine

'It has to stop,' said Mum at last. She was sitting on the end of my bed, looking tired and defeated. She was talking about going swimming. I was panicking.

'But I need to exercise!'

'Not like this.'

'I have to!'

Round and round. But she won me over by looking suddenly very crushed and saying, 'I don't know, Jessica. I don't know if I can do this. I just despair, sometimes, of you ever getting any better.'

That scared me. I couldn't be alone, so – 'I'll stop swimming.' Simple words. To me, lead weights.

Monday came, a day when I usually swam. I walked about in a frenzy:

'*Got to go, got to go—*'

'*No. No. Only confusion that way.*'

So I held myself in check. That was progress, in a sense, but it was sad, because I used to like swimming and it was the one sport I was any good at. Mum and I took a walk in the park together instead. We were OK. We had a new plan.

Meanwhile I kept seeing Sarah and the practice nurse. My weight stayed just about the same. I breezed through school, not applying myself in the slightest and usually distracted by obsessions. I did the work with the barest amount of attention. It was too easy for me. The novelty of hospitalization had worn off and I was no longer a celebrity. The kids just thought me weird. The distance from my old friends didn't close up. We were different now. We were all changed.

The only lesson that did matter was PE. Here was my sole remaining chance of fitness. They were starting to stress fitness as an aim for teenage girls; and this included taking our pulse between bouts of exercise to check our heart rate got up high enough. More numbers for the Monkey to manipulate. I remember standing in the gym, two fingers anxiously pressed to my throat – was it fast enough? Was I pushing myself too little now? How lazy! I kept miscounting—

'Jess, what are you doing?' The others gave me weird looks. I ignored them and ran to the teacher.

'Miss, Miss – I think I did it wrong, can I do it again?'

I was not doing gym for much longer.

In the middle of June, Sarah left the practice at the clinic. It was nearly time to have her baby; then she would be working in another part of the country. I was sad as I had grown very fond of her. I thanked her for all her help and wished her the best for the future. From now on, she said, I'd have appointments with a psychiatric nurse. This nurse proved to be an uninterested and uninteresting woman who could never take Sarah's place. I closed my mouth and mind to her within five minutes of our meeting, and missed sessions whenever I could.

chapter ten

Summer brought the SATS. I had forgotten what day
they were scheduled until I got to school. We pupils
were shown into the sports hall and the papers doled
out. I sat down, picked up my pen and did the papers.

I knew the answers in maths and science: I had read
a couple of textbooks in the unit. I made up the English.
I enjoyed the peace of the exams. The pupils were quiet;
the large space of the dusty hall now lined with desks
impressed them. I finished early, then sat and watched
the dust motes dancing in the sunbeams through high
windows, and re-read the graffiti on my desk.

'End of test.'

I passed my paper to the front and left. I didn't give
a damn what I'd got. I was not surprised when I found
out I'd achieved top levels; nor was I particularly pleased.
I already knew I was clever. Sometimes I wished I was
duller: I could not see a Monkey surviving inside a slow
brain. There wouldn't be enough to feed on.

I didn't bother going to many lessons after the SATS finished. It was nearly time for the summer holidays. Nothing was happening in the lessons – just scraps and paper aeroplanes. I spent a lot of time in the learning-support unit, reading novels. I was on file as having 'emotional difficulties' and could go there whenever I wanted. I was thinking of food less – and living in a state of baffled, sad calm. The end of the school year came and went.

Now the days were long and warm and empty. I took a lot of walks, alone. I wasn't even compelled to run. Bees buzzed, collecting nectar from the open flowers, and my mind took on a similar lazy hum. That far-off day, when I was trying to do sit-ups on the bedroom floor, when the GP came and stood above me, she had said something that made no sense at the time. She said that, in reality, we know very little about mental illness. But the mind is like the body in one way at least: sometimes it gets damaged. And in the end, all we can really do, at least for now, is foster the right conditions for healing of the mind to come about and give the patient support while it happens. My mind had indeed been damaged. Now I wondered if this buzz was like the sore, dim buzz of pain that means an open wound is healing.

My grandmother was still living in a nursing home nearby, and Mum continued to visit her frequently. Over the summer I began to accompany her sometimes. Nan didn't scare me now. She was not in our world. She lived in a small room, a bed on one side and a wardrobe, and sat in a green chair that reclined or straightened at the touch of a button. Near the chair was a tray, always covered with sweeties and cakes and bananas. Nonetheless she was very thin. Sometimes the room smelled bad. They were supposed to keep old people clean, but they were overworked and understaffed. That sounded very familiar. Old nurses who did not care and young ones who did not know what to do.

Nan had grown smaller and wrinkled and very grey. Sometimes she seemed half asleep and didn't know we were there. Sometimes she would shout and say things that did not make sense, converse with her long-dead husband or sister. Other times, she'd have a moment of amazing clarity, like looking over at this big clock that my uncle got for her and saying clearly: 'The time now is quarter to three,' which it actually was. I would sit there in her little room, usually on the bed, while my mum did her hair in big rollers. Nan's hands were like blue-veined spiders.

My nan did small, pathetic things. Arranging and

re-arranging the few items on the little table just in front of her. And she always had to hold onto her bag. I used to keep arranging things in my room. And all her life, they say, she had worried. Just like me. So was this where I was headed? This fraught non-life they called dementia? I kept finding excuses to go out of the room, fetching a teacup or taking it back. I went into the lounge and played the piano.

And I was jealous – I admit it. Because of all the patience that my mother showed with her own mother, who was also nasty sometimes, while I felt unappreciated, snapped at, shoved aside. In my diary I raged over arguments. Sadness and self-punishment gave way to anger and frustration; the cry was no longer '*I'm wicked*' but '*What's wrong with them all?*' The naïve little girl who took every slight to heart was gone. In her place was a moody teenager raging at her family, the world and everything.

I might not have my period, but it looked like I'd hit puberty at last.

chapter eleven

It was a peculiar summer. One thing we don't lack in our family is money. Not that we're rich, but we're comfortable, and that year my mother bought a caravan in Tenby, West Wales. Tenby's a lovely place in summer. Blue sea, blue sky, golden sand. Cute and poky village shops not totally smothered by tourism, terraced houses in pastel colours. Sometimes we went in a group with Erica, my mother's friend, and her two sons, Ian and Billy. Ian is my age and Billy's a couple of years younger. They're good fun. There's no hidden agenda, not a malicious bone in any of them. I can be myself around them, and it's genuine. We have real conversations and we play good games and take the piss out of each other without worry. They don't get offended or spiteful so easily. With Erica and Ian and Billy I relax.

Anyway, we had some good times in the caravan; they came down with us for weekends, and we made campfires out the front and toasted marshmallows. I ate three.

Billy tried to brand Adam with his marshmallow stick and chased him round the caravan one evening, while Ian and I fell about laughing.

There were bad times, too. The boys played football on the beach and I ran around, randomly trying to burn up calories. There wasn't even any point to it; because if I lost weight I knew I'd only have to eat more. It was just automatic, second nature. Then there was the time my mother took me to the village shops, and I tried on a pair of size eight trousers: the cut did not suit me, and the back seams pulled. I went back to the caravan, shut myself in the bedroom, and argued with the Monkey. She was crooning, '*COME BACK TO ME, BABY. I'LL TREAT YOU REAL GOOD.*'

'*No. I am getting my life back.*'

'*YOU'VE REALLY LET YOURSELF GO, YOU KNOW. SIZE EIGHT DON'T EVEN FIT.*'

'*It wasn't the size, it was the cut. Other size eights fit me with space in. The only way I'd get those trousers to fit would be to lose so much weight my bum disappeared, which would be really unhealthy.*'

'*BURN CALORIES, YOU FAT LAZY BITCH! GET UP! MOVE!*'

I did some sit-ups on the bedroom floor, but then they were not good enough so I had to do them again.

Eventually I stopped. I wasn't satisfied, I was in pain. I imagined forcing down the Monkey, composed myself and came out, smiling painfully.

Another weekend in Tenby, we took a boat trip from the beach over the bay to Caldey Island and its monastery. Sometimes in summer the sky is a real deep blue. A bright sun shines on Caldey and lights the green grass up beyond the cliffs. Flowers dot the fields, and rocky paths go winding up to the island's heights. Small waterfalls come trickling down into pools. There, if you can block your ears to the sounds of tourists on the grass flats, you can wander a while and watch the water dance and feel like the first person on earth. In the winter, the cliffs are stark and black against a steel sky, the water churns, and the gull-song is piercing. The trees are bleak and barren. It's a good place for a monastery; no one would doubt a power up there.

Though there are more buildings up on Caldey for the tourists now, they are quaint and rustic, to grate as little as possible against the majestic scenery. Cobblestone paths and tea gardens with sunshades, serving tea and monk-made scones and jam.

Our trip was for half a day. I did not speak on the way there. I was far away, and the others sensibly ignored me. But the island affected me as it always did, and on the boat ride back a strange thing happened.

I was sitting near the side and watching the foam go churning past, the shrinking island standing on the water. I felt a profound sense of loss and asked, *Where is God?* and then a voice inside my head said, '*Jump out.*'

It was the Monkey – I recognized her at once, though the tone was different. She was playing sneak now, coaxing and beguiling. She slipped me a beautiful notion: if I jumped out of the boat I'd swim away, free as the seals and gulls, be one with nature and the water and leave the human world behind me with its sickness, its complexity and grief. The desire, and the mad conviction this was possible, was so strong that I had to grip the boat side to restrain myself, remember all the terrible sea stories I'd ever heard, and grit my teeth until the passage ended and my feet were safely back on sand. The fact that I did that taught me a lesson. As I stepped out and felt firm land beneath me, I knew with absolute and strengthening conviction that *I wanted to live my life.*

Something was happening, subtly, surely. I think it was called perspective. The desperation was going, fading, and with it the terror of the illness. Lying in bed, one night back at home, and staring up into the darkness, I felt peace. I was not ecstatic and not overwhelmed with pleasure. But something big had

282

happened by degrees. It was a filtering out, like ink separating from water. I realized it with a jolt that physically moved my heart.

I did not need the Monkey any more.

She was not there. I could hear her absence in the silence. The Monkey is a crucial thing, a vibrant thing, a thing of intensity, fire. The fires were ashes. In their place: deflation. Quiet. I was tired, but no longer terrified. Because I had seen such bad things and survived them. What could hurt me now?

I ought to feel ecstasy. I didn't. I felt – emptiness. I had lost my tormentor. I had also lost my highs. I had lost my ally and my certainty; or perhaps I had at last seen through it, and known it for a traitor and a fraud.

Weeks passed calmly, quietly. I put on a few more pounds. It didn't matter. I went back to school.

It was not the same that year. Year Ten. So much older. Sometimes I had fun and laughed. The work was terribly easy. I was bored.

I was writing again. And I spent time chatting on the Internet. My friends were nice; but they didn't understand me. They were from another time, friends of the old unreal me, scared of the beast in me and hardly daring to believe it could be put away. That saddened me. I needed to start a new time.

chapter twelve

'Jess,' said Adam, 'I gotta book you should read.'

It was December. The autumn had gone so fast. When I was small, and looking forward to Christmas desperately, I used to wish I could just fall asleep and wake up to find that Christmas had come. This year it felt like it was almost happening. The older you get, the faster time goes, they say. The approaching season filled me with a mixture of dread and horror and bitter pride, remembering the circumstances last year. Also gratitude. A lot of gratitude. So I would see another Christmas.

'What kind of book?'

'Well, it's a fantasy.'

My nose wrinkled. 'Don't like fantasy really.'

'Go on. It's a really good book.'

'Oh yeah? What's it about?'

'A ring. Well, no.' He paused. 'Not *about* a ring as such. There's a ring in it. It's more about – well, really,

Jess, you have to read it for yourself. But it's really good.'

What the heck. A book's a book and I was bored. If I didn't like it I'd just stop.

The book was Tolkien's *The Lord of the Rings*, which in Adam's edition had 1008 pages. I began it on a Monday morning and finished it, stunned, on Thursday afternoon. I was utterly mesmerized. I forgot about diet, exercise, fatness, thinness, monkeys and psychiatric units. Granted, I did not do much else for those four days, but I didn't regret that for a moment. Now, I'm not one of these crazy people – quite – who claim that that book is the Ultimate Truth of the Universe. At the time I didn't even know it had all these awards like 'Book of the Century' or whatever. It was simply what I needed when I needed it, and it shoved the Monkey from my head for the duration of my reading with a total and complete efficiency.

I think *The Lord of the Rings* wrung just about every emotion I have out of me. I did not believe in every theory, every idea in it, but I got the gist. Love is the most powerful thing, more powerful than death. Friendship is strong, people are good; but at the end of the day, you're on your own. Don't panic! Nothing lasts for ever in this world, just try your best, just try your very hardest, cos there's no point in despair; and things will be OK in the end. It also gave me a hypoth-esis for Evil I could work with. I had been wondering what it was, and how it worked, and why God let it, and the book told me to forget that. The point is that there *is* Evil, even if Evil means the absence of something, like love. And there is God in the book, but He didn't appear in the sky and say, '*Now I shall punish you!*' or '*Now listen up while I tell you what to do.*'

All that mattered to me. But something mattered more. Or should I say *someone*.

When I read about Gollum sitting rocking in the darkness, arguing with the strong voice in his head . . . when he felt he needed that voice to survive, and if he could just touch the Ring, then sod it all, everything would be fine . . . when he grovelled, pleaded or screamed and lashed out in a sudden rage . . . when he was overcome with sadness and despair and sheer life-sucking *tiredness* . . . then I realized.

I had found a monkey in a book.

So I was a Gollum. So I was not unique. And at last I realized how I appeared to other people. It did not even depress me that Gollum dies at the end, because the fact remained that *The Lord of the Rings* is fiction. That meant that someone else had known my kind of thoughts, had known my feelings and the torments of my mind, precisely and profoundly enough to invest them in a character. And of course, I then had a new hobby. One that was a damn sight more enjoyable than starvation.

So I started reading again with a vengeance. I read fantasy. And I wrote some. Then I read historical novels and myth and whatever else I could lay hands on. And I was happier, and looked outside myself, and I had fun with friends. My periods came back and I was pleased. Lighter days; I pretended I had not been ill, but I had, and I was new and different.

Year Ten passed, and I did my GCSEs. I didn't over-stress: I got eight A*s and two As and a B. Then I left high school without looking back, and I started college. Almost all the people there were new. I am OK, and my family are OK, and I want to go to university and be a writer when I grow up, not an anorexic. I eat well, and exercise – sanely. Sometimes I get very sad, especially when I think about the unit. I hated that place, but I liked the kids there, and I hope to God they all made it.

Insanity is like losing your path. It can happen to anybody, if their mood and circumstances are ripe for its cultivation. We really don't know much about it, and all we can do is help the person and support them till they find their own way back onto the path, if they can.

A very wise person once told me: 'No one is happy, Jessica. We all have happy times, and unhappy times, and neither stays for ever.'

Today my time is happy.

EPILOGUE:
TAMED

'Jessica!'

I was walking through the centre of town late one summer afternoon, when a loud, familiar shout from behind made me halt. I turned round.

'Chloe!' I screamed and flung myself into her arms. We stood there hugging for a long time, not bothered by the stares of passers-by. 'Oh my God, oh God,' I babbled as we broke apart. 'How are you? What are you doing?'

'I'm out, Jess, I'm out,' she almost sobbed, and we screamed and hugged all over again.

'So how are you?' we both said when we had our breath back, and then we both answered, 'I'm *fine.*'

I held her at arm's length and looked at her: 'But are you really fine?'

'Yes,' she said, and I knew she was telling the truth. There were no scratches on her face, her smile was real, and the pure relief in her voice told me all I needed to know. She looked young, but she told me she felt old, and I said I knew just what she was talking about.

'And the others?' I asked. 'Do you know anything?'

The smile faded from her face. 'Well, Robert's out,' she told me.

I nodded eagerly. 'I knew he'd be OK. I knew *you'd* be OK.'

'But I couldn't say about the others.'

'Sally? Manda?'

She knew nothing. 'But anyway,' she said, 'let's not go back there.'

She was right. It was not in my power to save the others; it had been a narrow thing saving myself. I was thrilled to know Chloe had made it. We exchanged a few more words, bits of news, then wished each other the best of luck and went our separate ways. The sun was going down, pink-gold and smudged along the sky before me. The evening air was fragrant, cool, my mind was clear, the grasping voice of madness broken, futile as the faintest breeze in leaves.

Author's Note

Monkey Taming is a work of fiction, but is inspired by my real experience of anorexia nervosa and time on a psychiatric unit. I am forever grateful to so many people for their help in my recovery, to the point that I can finally stand back and write this book – especially those other 'young people' I knew – not problem teenagers, but teenagers with problems, and quite honestly some of the nicest, most giving, intelligent and decent people I have ever known. Without their help, support and friendship, neither I nor *Monkey Taming* would be here today. I hope this book will encourage so-called 'normal' people to take a second look at those dubbed 'problematic', and shoved surreptitiously to the outskirts of society, regarded as useless, troublesome, even wicked. I hope it will help generate awareness of the traumas that have caused such people to behave the way they do, and of the light often concealed by the shadow of mental illness.

♪ A NOTE OF MADNESS

TABITHA SUZUMA

Why is this happening to me? he asked himself desperately. What is wrong with me? He pressed his fingers over his eyelids and took some rapid, shallow breaths. I can't bear this, he thought. I can't bear feeling like this. I can't bear living like this. I can't bear being me . . .

Life as a student is good for Flynn. As one of the top pianists at the Royal College of Music, he has been put forward for an important concert, the opportunity of a lifetime. But beneath the surface, things are changing. On a good day Flynn feels full of energy and life, but on a bad day being alive is worse than being dead. Sometimes he wants to compose and practise all night, at other times despair kicks in and he can't get out of bed. With the pressure of the forthcoming concert and the growing concern of his family and friends about his erratic behaviour and mood swings, emotions come to a head. Sometimes things can only get worse before they get better.

A convincingly complex and unsettling portrayal . . . Suzuma's compassion for her struggling hero makes for a genuinely moving read.' *Keith Gray*

'A gripping, brilliant, beautifully-written debut novel'
Annie Dalton

'A compulsively readable story . . . persuasive and admirable'
Jan Mark